Seed that Dies to Rise

Lenten Reflections on VOICES UNITED

Edited by John E. Ambrose

THE UNITED CHURCH PUBLISHING HOUSE

Seed that Dies to Rise

Canadian Cataloguing in Publication Data

Main entry under title:
Seed that dies to rise: Lenten reflections on Voices United

Includes bibliographical references.
ISBN 1-55134-067-4

1. Lent - Prayer-books and devotions - English.
2. Lenten hymns. I. Ambrose, John E. (John Edward), 1936-

BV85.S415 1997 242'.34 C96-932522-3

The United Church Publishing House
3250 Bloor St. West, 4th floor
Etobicoke, Ontario, Canada
M8X 2Y4
(416) 231-5931

Printed in Canada

960451

Contents

Week Six

Week Seven

Introduction

It was one of those insightful mistakes. The workshop leader had two burgundy-coloured books on the table in front of him. Without looking down, he selected one of the books, held it up before the group, and said, "This is the church's first and most essential resource for the nurturing of faith." The puzzled look on the faces of the people prompted him to glance at what he was holding. It was *Voices United.* He had intended to pick up the Bible. "Whoops," he said. "Let me try that again." What he wanted to point out was that *next to the Bible,* a hymn book is a congregation's most important resource for the nurture and development of faith. For some in the gathering, it was no mistake. Hymns were indeed central to their growth in faith and discipleship, in some ways more directly influential than scripture.

The lenten reflections in this booklet are based on hymns found in *Voices United.* The writers have made their own choices, resulting in a cross-section of hymns from different periods, different countries, and of different styles. All of the authors have served in various areas of ministry—pastoral, teaching, music, mission—and bring these experiences to their comments. The reflections are rich with personal stories, with insights into the struggles of faith, and with Christian hope. We visit places we have not been, and engage with experiences we may not have personally known. The result is a wonderful mix of theological insight, witness to deep faith, compassion for human need, and a love of hymnody.

This booklet will serve well for personal or group devotion. Readers are encouraged to turn to *Voices United* and to read—or sing—the hymns in their entirety. Several hymns were chosen by more than one author. These duplications have been retained because they show so beautifully how hymns speak differently to different people.

May the thoughts and stories of others lead you to deeper reflection on your own experiences of life and faith, and of the hymns of life and faith, during this season of Lent.

John E. Ambrose

Theme Hymn

TREE OF LIFE AND AWESOME MYSTERY

Tree of life and awesome mystery,
in your death we are reborn,
though you die in all of history,
still you rise with every morn,
still you rise with every morn.

Seed that dies to rise in glory,
may we see ourselves in you,
if we learn to live your story
we may die to rise anew,
we may die to rise anew.

We remember truth once spoken,
love passed on through act and word,
every person lost and broken
wears the body of our Lord,
wears the body of our Lord.

Gentle Jesus, mighty Spirit,
come inflame our hearts anew,
we may all your joy inherit
if we bear the cross with you,
if we bear the cross with you.

Christ, you lead and we shall follow,
stumbling though our steps may be,
one with you in joy and sorrow,
we the river, you the sea,
we the river, you the sea.

Theme Hymn

Verses for Lent

General
Light of life beyond conceiving,
mighty Spirit of our Lord;
give new strength to our believing,
give us faith to live your word,
give us faith to live your word.

First Sunday
From the dawning of creation,
you have loved us as your own;
stay with us through all temptation,
make us turn to you alone,
make us turn to you alone.

Second Sunday
In our call to be a blessing,
may we be a blessing true;
may we live and die confessing
Christ as Lord of all we do,
Christ as Lord of all we do.

Third Sunday
Living Water of salvation,
be the fountain of each soul;
springing up in new creation,
flow in us and make us whole,
flow in us and make us whole.

Fourth Sunday
Give us eyes to see you clearly,
make us children of your light;
give us hearts to live more nearly
as your gospel shining bright,
as your gospel shining bright.

Fifth Sunday
God of all our fear and sorrow,
God who lives beyond our death;
hold us close through each tomorrow,
love as near as every breath,
love as near as every breath.

Marty Haugen, 1984
Voices United, 121

Ash Wednesday

Sunday's Palms Are Wednesday's Ashes (1)

Laura Sundberg

Verse 1

Sunday's palms are Wednesday's ashes
as another Lent begins;
thus we kneel before our Maker
in contrition for our sins.
We have marred baptismal pledges,
in rebellion gone astray;
now, returning, seek forgiveness;
grant us pardon, God, this day!

Rae E. Whitney, 1982
Voices United, 107

It was Ash Wednesday 1995. I sat at the table with the youth confirmation class. Like many United Church people, they had never heard of Ash Wednesday. I could see their eyes widen with curiosity when I told them we were going to set palms on fire!

The dried palm fronds before us were from last year's Palm Sunday service. Someone struck a match, and we began the slow process of burning. Palms are stubborn. A couple of inches burned, fell into the urn, then the flame went out. We were left with a woody fibre. A pleasant, woody smell filled the air.

The palms had turned to ashes before our eyes. Their stubborn transformation reminded me of the act of repentance itself.

Repentance is an act of turning, of change, of conversion. When we sin, it is as if we turn away from God's ways, from God's desire for us and for our world. When we do this, we turn away from one another's needs as well. In our turning away from God, we also often turn away from our own needs.

Ash Wednesday is a day of repentance. We come with our hurts, our fears and stand open and vulnerable before our Maker. We come admitting those wrongs we have done to ourselves and others. We come, asking God's help in changing.

The palm ashes remind us of not only our individual, but our collective need for repentance. The palms were waved by a cheering crowd. It was also a crowd that turned on Jesus, demanding his crucifixion.

The fire of Ash Wednesday is God's transforming power, the power of Jesus' gift of courage, strength, love for us and for the world.

The teens and I spoke together about repentance. I invited them to come to God to confess their sins, and to ask God for help in changing their lives. Together, in silence, we made our confession. Then we wrote a prayer that named something that we wanted to give up to God's transforming power. We burned these papers as a cleansing, an offering, a sign of our willingness to change.

As the papers burned, the natural smell of the palms was replaced by the foul smell of burning paper. I imagined that this smell of repentance was more pleasing to God than incense.

We mixed the ashes together with a few drops of water. We turned to one another, marking one another with the sign of the cross. We sent one another out, to love, to serve.

For Prayer

We come to you this day, O God, open to your transforming fire. Burn away that which keeps us from being vulnerable and open to you. Help us to turn to one another as we journey together this lenten season. Amen.

Thursday

Sunday's Palms Are Wednesday's Ashes (2)

Fran Ota

Verse 3

We are hasty to judge others,
blind to proof of human need;
and our lack of understanding
demonstrates our inner greed;
we have wasted earth's resources;
want and suffering we've ignored;
come and cleanse us, then restore us;
make new hearts within us, Lord.

Rae E. Whitney, 1982
Voices United, 107

"No more shall the sound of weeping be heard in it, or the cry of distress. No more shall there be in it an infant that lives but a few days, or an old person who does not live out a lifetime...." (Isa. 65:19b–20a)

In the spring of 1972, two young women sat in an ice cream parlour in the gentle tropical Saigon afternoon, savouring the sunshine and the rich ice cream. A girl not much more than sixteen approached them. She carried a baby two or three months old, born with a cleft palate—but the cleft had been further mutilated, to make the baby as pathetic as possible. One young woman wanted to take the baby to the hospital; her Vietnamese friend stopped her. "It's money they need; otherwise they will just take the child home and do the same thing again. It is hard, but you must give her money, nothing else."

That one young woman was me—26, with a baby of my own also three months old, at home being minded by a nanny. I sat up all that night holding my beautiful, healthy son, crying and wondering about a God that allowed him to be born even in wartime, in the best hospital with the best doctors, while another mother had to mutilate her child in order to live. We were the privileged diplomatic class, covered by four different embassies, spending weekends in a colonial hotel villa on the snow-white sands of Vung Tau beach.

What a contrast to the lives of the Vietnamese! My husband's students died on the battlefield. From the organ bench at the airbase chapel I saw men cry to go home, and the next week saw them go out in a body bag. Defoliants, dumped on the "wrong village by mistake," drifted back over Saigon, and one by one the elegant old elms began to die. People died of cholera, typhoid, and cancer; some suffered ectopic pregnancies; war injuries were the number ten cause of death. Speculation was that the war was about offshore oil rights; whatever the reasons, Vietnam was only the arena in which the war was fought.

Rubber plantations, a major source of income, were destroyed. The food chain has been compromised for eternity. Mine sweepers are needed before crops can be planted. Rice crop yields remain lower than their pre-war level—yet Vietnam used to supply all of southeast Asia. The overt war may have ended, but the toll in human life continues.

For Prayer

God our Mother, you weep at the cleaving and mutilation of creation. We are shamed. We may not have lifted the gun, nor dropped the chemicals, but we are complicit in having allowed it to happen. How often will we say "never again," then tacitly watch as it does? Release us from the paralyzing fear of standing out, and give us the strength and compassion to speak as individuals and as a church. We have been silent too long. In the name of Jesus your son we pray. Amen.

Friday

A Light Is Gleaming

Donna Sinclair

Refrain

A light is gleaming,
spreading its arms throughout the night,
living in the light.
Come share its gladness,
God's radiant love is burning bright,
living in the light.

Linnea Good, 1992
Voices United, 82

To the old German mystics, says theologian Dorothee Soelle, light was a favoured name for God. She likes this very much; "light" is not bound by class or gender. It is not a symbol of power; we simply belong—not submit—to God.

I love the way God-as-light suffuses this hymn, calling me to live in unity with God ("living in the light") in the fashion of those ancient mystics.

The image speaks to me as one of a winter people, one who burns candles, miniature symbols of the sun. Each morning I wait for the slow winter dawn to burn away the night; it always arrives, an assured miracle, slanting gold across the snow outside my windows, warming my house, "spreading its arms throughout the night." Who could not believe, in the face of this daily visitation by a blazing God desiring only to warm "all our days"?

So this new hymn searches ancient roots, coaxing hope from the frozen ground of this century, feeding it with half-forgotten images. God as light, calling me out of the darkness of shattered institutions, hurting my eyes at first, yes, the way the winter sun on snow dazzles in the beginning. But I live here, in the promise of spring. And "living in the light" I live as the mystics did, in God.

For Prayer

Thank you for your light, O God,
your radiant love. Amen.

Saturday

O Love That Wilt Not Let Me Go

Ian MacLean

Verse 3

O Joy that seekest me through pain,
I cannot close my heart to thee;
I trace the rainbow through the rain,
and feel the promise is not vain
that morn shall tearless be.

George Matheson, 1881
Voices United, 658

Someone who reads this will help me I'm sure. Who is (or was) it who talks about "not around or over or under, but through"—as in "Yea, though I walk through the valley...." Maybe it was Edgar Guest whose poems are loaded with self-determination and the values and rewards thereof. There is hint of the resolution in phrases like, "he set his face to go to Jerusalem" (Luke 9:51). But there is a difference. "If it be possible, let this cup pass...nevertheless, not my will but thine...." Or, to finish the line from the shepherd's psalm... "for thou art with me, thy rod and thy staff they comfort (in the original 'with power') me." They empower me.

"O love that wilt not let me go..." George Matheson wrote out of his blindness and brokenheartedness. The woman he loved had just delivered her "Dear George" letter. His blindness, and the bleak future it forewarned, was more than she bargained for. She wanted him (or someone) "for better, not for worse." That's when, in his misery and pain he wrote, "O love that wilt not let me go...I trace the rainbow through the rain"—the rain of his own tears. Have you never noticed that phenomenon? It may be through tears, or tired eyes, or wind in your face, but suddenly the "clear" light is fractured into the colours of the rainbow—like those strange summer days when it's raining over there and sunny over here—and water bends the beam of light into glorious colour. A mixed blessing.

The theme hymn (p. 1) says "Christ, you lead and we shall follow, stumbling though our steps may be, one with you in joy and sorrow, we the river, you the sea." And Matheson wrote, "I give thee back the life I owe, that in thine ocean depths its flow may richer, fuller be." And we still at times sing the Medical Mission Sisters song, "I saw raindrops on my window, joy is like the rain, laughter runs across my pain..." or pain is woven through our laughter. Ah, this is more than "stiff upper lip," "damn the torpedoes, full speed ahead" bravery. This is courage. From the French *coeur*, from the Latin *cor*, meaning "heart." Not the strong heart, but the broken heart. The broken heart restored by the mercy of God. The heart of one who himself "was a man of sorrow and acquainted with grief." It is the simplicity beyond complicity. I don't know who first said this, but I heard it from Robert Raines, "I wouldn't give a plugged nickel for simplicity this side of complexity, but I would give everything for the simplicity the other side of complexity," where love is—love that never lets us go.

For Prayer

A thought: think for a moment. Can you name your pain? Think some more.... What joy is struggling to be born? Breathe deeply...push!

1st Sunday in Lent

With Joy We Meditate

Mac Watts

Verse 2

Touched with a sympathy within,
he [Christ] knows our feeble frame;
he knows what sore temptations mean,
for he has felt the same.

Isaac Watts
Voices United, 351

A friend of mine is a member of Alcoholics Anonymous. He told me of the circumstances of attending his first AA meeting. Another friend of his dragged him kicking and screaming to the meeting, and got him only barely inside the door, where he stood, refusing to take a chair. The only good thing he could think of about the place was that it was full of cigarette smoke, and he leaned against the wall with a cigarette in his mouth defying anybody to try to convert him. But nobody did. Instead the meeting started, and the person in the chair said, "My name is John, and I am an alcoholic." After going through some business items, he introduced a speaker who was dressed like a construction worker and hadn't bothered to go home to change his clothes. The man said, "My name is Larry, and I am an alcoholic," and then followed up with the story of a life of uncontrolled drinking, until he was finally brought by a pal to an AA meeting. My friend says he hardly noticed himself moving toward a chair and sitting down. He was among people who lived where he lived. Larry's story, and the stories of those who spoke after he did, were so much like his own he could hardly believe it. Nobody tried to convert him that night, but it happened all the same.

In most of our portrayals of Jesus he is held up in his perfections. Even when we talk about his love, kindness, and compassion we are noting his perfections, and in so doing we are not all wrong but may nevertheless be placing him sufficiently above us that we can't imagine him ever standing where we stand, or feeling what we feel. Yet that was what the writer to the Hebrews wanted so desperately to make clear. "Therefore he had to become like his brothers and sisters *in every respect,* so that he might be a merciful and faithful high priest in the service of God, to make a sacrifice of atonement for the sins of the people. Because he himself was tested by what he suffered, he is able to help those who are being tested." (Heb. 2:17–18) "For we do not have a high priest who is unable to sympathize with our weaknesses, but we have one who in every respect has been tested as we are, yet without sin. Let us therefore approach the throne of grace with boldness, so that we may receive mercy and find grace to help in time of need." (Heb. 4:15–16)

Many of us have been conditioned to identify sinlessness with moral elevation, and someone morally elevated feels uncomfortable with those lagging behind, or the latter uncomfortable in his or her presence. If we attribute to Jesus a moral elevation that makes him uncomfortable with imperfect people, we are not talking of the real Jesus. When the apostolic writers said that Jesus was without sin, they were not referring to moral rectitude, but to the fact that Jesus' trust in God and self-giving to others was unreserved, untainted by ego. He chose to stand where we stand, and thus he felt what we feel. And therefore he reaches out to us, saying, "Come to me, all you that are weary and are carrying heavy burdens, and I will give you rest. Take my yoke upon you, and learn from me; for I am gentle and humble in heart, and you will find rest for your souls. For my yoke is easy, and my burden is light." (Matt. 11:28–30)

Monday

To the Desert Jesus Came

Stephen Adams

Verse 1

To the desert Jesus came,
to wrestle and to seek God's way.
Sun and moon rose high above
to watch him as he'd fast and pray.
Together through the valley,
the tempter led him around.
Together through the valley,
so Jesus answers found.

Linnea Good, 1992
Voices United, 113

There is always something shocking about the notion that Jesus was tempted at all. Wasn't he the Messiah, the son of God, one of the persons of the Trinity? And yet we are told that he "wrestled" with the tempter.

Did the tempter ever have a chance, really, offering Jesus such mundane lures as physical comfort, or power over other people? We recognize, uncomfortably, how difficult these same tests are for ourselves—but for the Messiah? Even the impulse to proclaim himself from the pinnacle of the temple does not sound like something Jesus would seriously consider, even though it would merely be using questionable means to achieve "a win-win situation."

T.S. Eliot, in his play *Murder in the Cathedral*, portrays a similar

For Prayer

O God, you are light to the lost, bread to the hungry, deliverance to the captive, healing to the sick, eternal vision to the dying, and harbour to every soul in peril. Gather the wanderers from every corner of the world into the community of your mercy and grace, that we may eternally praise you for our salvation in Jesus Christ our Lord. Amen.*

**Daily Prayer, Book of Common Worship. Westminster/John Knox: 1993, p. 338.*

temptation. Thomas à Becket, knowing he faces martyrdom in defence of the church, confronts three tempters, who offer him escape from his dilemma, political power, even the means to benefit his beloved people—and Thomas fends them off easily. But then comes a fourth, unexpected, who catches him off guard: he makes Thomas the most subtle offer of all, the glory of the very martyrdom he anticipates. Thomas will go to his death in full knowledge of his own spiritual superiority.

Jesus' most serious temptation, perhaps, was to behave not like a man but like a magician, and that would be to throw off the humanity that makes him like us. God may be within each of us, but that does not make each of us a god; and persons who behave like God (we all know one or two) are apt to seem less than godlike in other ways.

For ourselves, we do resist temptation from time to time, but rarely the temptation to congratulate ourselves for doing so. We pray for a God of magic solutions. But Jesus in the desert chose the hard way: to remain human and to conduct his ministry from a position of powerlessness until the inevitable end, not only in agony but humiliation.

FOR PRAYER

Lead us not into temptation, God,but give us strength and courage to follow your example. Deliver us from evils of our own making. Forgive us our grave failings, and lead us to believe we are forgiven so that we are not disabled by remorse. And let our trust in your comprehensive mercy teach us how to forgive others. Amen

Tuesday

Let Us Talents and Tongues Employ

Bob Wallace

Verse 1

Let us talents and tongues employ,
reaching out with a shout of joy:
bread is broken, the wine is poured,
Christ is spoken and seen and heard.

Refrain

Jesus lives again, earth can breathe again,
pass the Word around: loaves abound!

Fred Kaan, 1975
Voices United, 468

Musician *extraordinaire*, the late Doreen Potter introduced the churches of the world to one another's music. As wife of the General Secretary of the World Council of Churches, Philip Potter, she was in a unique position to do so. Her early death robbed the world church of her talent, but she left us a legacy. She edited Cantate Domino, the World Council's multilingual song book, one of the first collections of modern church music on a global scale. She also left a number of her own compositions. One of the most original is her arrangement of a Jamaican calypso melody from her husband's Caribbean heritage. Colleague and companion at the Council, Fred Kaan, author of many hymns in *Voices United*, contributed the lyrics to produce, "Let us talents and tongues employ." The hymn was first sung at the Council's Assembly in Nairobi in 1975 with author and composer leading. Let the bongos, maracas, and wood blocks sound in your imagination as the catchy calypso rhythm carries the text.

Our lenten devotions include taking the measure of our own talents and seeing the degree to which we are allowing them to be employed by God's spirit. Christians often find it hard to be realistic about their talents. There is the impression that to recognize one's gifts is to be boastful. True humility, however, is not putting oneself down, but standing at full height, appreciating the gifts we can bring to our work and to our daily encounters, "reaching out with a shout of joy."

The hymn speaks of "talents and tongues." D.T. Niles of Sri Lanka described the Christian faith as "one beggar telling another where bread is to be found." If we are hesitant about acknowledging talent, we are probably even more reticent about acknowledging our faith to others. Telling or "witnessing" is one of faith's essential disciplines. It may be with a shout of joy, or with a quiet word of direction so that in us "Christ is spoken, and seen and heard."

Wednesday

Now Quit Your Care

For Prayer
Creator and Nurturer, we are grateful for talents and tongues, vocals and vocations. These are your gifts and we would use each to your glory. Amen.

Fran Ota

Verse 2
To bow the head in sackcloth and in ashes,
or rend the soul, such grief is not Lent's goal;
but to be led to where God's glory flashes,
God's beauty to come near.
Make clear, make clear,
make clear where truth and light appear.

Percy Dearmer, 1928
Voices United, 109

"For I desire steadfast love and not sacrifice, the knowledge of God rather than burnt offerings." (Hos. 6:6) "By people of strange tongues and by the lips of foreigners I will speak to this people; yet even then they will not listen to me...." (1 Cor. 14:21)

Our small family group sat on chairs facing the temple altar. As the priest repeated the phrase "Na mu a mi da butsu"—which roughly translates as "We call upon your name, O Buddha"—each of us went to the altar, sprinkled a few grains of incense on a brazier, and prayed for Otoosan.* The priest had chosen that phrase purposely, he said, out of respect for the Christians who were there—it has much the same meaning as "Amen." As we prayed, there was a definite palpable presence in the room, and God was there as much as in any Christian church.

My husband's family is a pretty mixed bag. There are a couple of Protestants and Catholics, some Buddhists and some who have no religious faith at all. Two cousins have married Europeans and live outside of Japan. It is because of this intercultural and interfaith life experience that the scriptures and hymn verse have such importance for me.

Many cultural and religious groups use ashes or smoke in some way. Native peoples purify themselves with smoke from sacred plants; Hindus purify with the smoke from burnt entrails of sacred animals; during Lent Christians use the smoke and ashes from the palm crosses of the previous year's Palm Sunday.

Is the point *where* God speaks, or *how*? Is God more present in Christian churches or Buddhist temples? Is God interested in how correctly we sprinkle the incense, rend our clothes, or mark ourselves with ashes—or is God more interested in knowledge, wisdom, and love? Which is more important—to dress up in sackcloth and ashes, burn palm crosses, and observe the outward trappings of Lent, or to spend time reflecting on the world God created, and the ashes we create by our greed, selfishness, or blindness to the many places where God's truth and light can be found?

For Prayer

O God of wisdom, reflection, and knowledge, we call upon your name. We cry out to you in anguish and need. It is so easy to go through the motions, to "give up" something, and pat ourselves on the back for our fortitude; it is more difficult to spend time reflecting. Our vision is narrow—yours is broad; we choose the obvious easy path, you ask us to take the one less used. Help us in this season of Lent, to find your truth, and to come closer to knowing how to love as you love. We pray in the name of Jesus, who wrestled with human temptations and chose the less travelled road. Amen.

**Otoosan: Japanese honorific word meaning "father."*

Thursday

The Lone Wild Bird

Laura Sundberg

Verse 1

The lone wild bird in lofty flight
is still with you, nor leaves your sight.
And I am yours! I rest in you,
Great Spirit, come, rest in me too.
Henry Richard McFadyen, 1925
Voices United, 384

The Qu'Appelle Valley is one of the many gifts of God to Saskatchewan. As one drives across the prairie, it appears suddenly, without warning.

One summer's day I was travelling up the south face of the valley near the native community of Lebret. I was travelling with Wes, one of the local funeral directors. We were returning from an interment at the Fort Qu'Appelle Cemetery.

The road at Lebret is steep, gravelled, with a sharp turn at the top. This was the first time I had been on the road. Even though I was a passenger, my eyes were straight ahead, on the road. I could just imagine a sudden disaster if another car met us head on, on the curve.

Wes, however, had driven the road countless times. He was familiar enough with the road to take a moment to look at the view as we ascended. The hills rose gently on the far side, green with the season's rain. The Qu'Appelle River made its way through the valley, as it emptied from Katepwa Lake nearby. It shimmered blue, reflecting the prairie sky. The fields below were green. As he looked out on the valley, he pointed out a sight that will stay with me for the rest of my life. There was an eagle, soaring on the air currents.

The lone eagle repeatedly dipped and soared on the air currents. Isaiah came to mind:

> But those who wait for the Lord shall renew their strength, they shall mount up with wings like eagles, they shall run and not be weary, they shall walk and not faint. (Isa. 40:31)

As I watched, I felt such a sense of freedom. It was as if the eagle was soaring on the air currents of the Spirit, upheld by God's love.

Lent is a season in which we need to be reminded that we are upheld by God's care. We can feel the heavy load of our inward journey; of our world's seeming denial of God's way of justice, peace, love, and compassion. In the midst of it all God says, "You are mine, and I am yours. You are not alone."

In Lent, we often stress the inner journey. Although we look inward, we do not do it alone. I would not have seen the eagle without Wes pointing it out to me. I was so focused on the road, on getting to the top, on possible problems ahead, that I was not able to look around. I would have missed this reminder of God's presence without him.

God upholds us on our lenten journey through our companions on the way, our companions in faith, our companions in life, our companions in the creation.

FOR PRAYER

O God, we give you thanks that you send us companions on the way. O friend and companion Jesus, we give you thanks that you uphold us on our journey. Help us to companion one another this lenten season. Help us to companion the earth. Amen.

Friday

WHEN WE ARE TEMPTED TO DENY YOUR SON

Stephen Adams

VERSE 1

When we are tempted to deny your Son,
because we fear the anger of the world,
and we are few who bear the insults hurled,
your will, O God, be done.

David W. Romig, 1965
Voices United, 119

When was the last time I said in public "I am a Christian"? I murmur it in church on Sundays, but when during daily life? This hymn begins, "When we are tempted to deny your Son, because we fear the anger of the world," and we are reminded that Christians are no longer the dominant group in our society, however we may behave. The image of the church is tarnished. Religion is no longer supposed to enter everyday life. As a teacher, I may admit that "I am a Christian" once in a while, but questions would be asked (and rightly so) if I said it too insistently.

We don't have to think back to the Inquisition and the burning of heretics to understand why the Christian church is subject to insults. There is plenty of disgrace today—from the misbehaviour of individual clergy, to the brazen demand for money by TV evangelists. But the abuses of power are not just individual, they are systemic. The church is splintered into bickering factions, each claiming a monopoly on the truth.

"Some keep the sabbath going to church," wrote Emily Dickinson. "I keep it staying home." One is tempted to follow her example. And yet, isn't living a Christian life "outside the church" the most extreme form of divisiveness? It might work for some. But for myself, it might mean a temptation to cultivate my own sense of superiority, treasuring a few comforting doctrines while ignoring others, setting up myself as the judge of God. Or it might just mean lapsing into spiritual apathy, assuming that my innate charity will survive on its own power.

No, when it's time to say "I am a Christian," it is saying that I am just one among many, who all have our individual gifts to bring, who all have our need for communion. The church, being a human institution, has many failings, but so do we all. And our paradoxical God somehow finds ways to use broken beings as instruments of good, if we open ourselves to the Spirit.

For Prayer

Eternal God, Creator of all things, we pray for renewed commitment to our community of faith, and the strength to weather the storms of doubt, apathy, or hostility. Give us the courage to speak our convictions in the world with forthrightness and humility, trusting in your holy word. Amen.

Saturday

I FEEL THE WINDS OF GOD TODAY

Jessie McLeod

VERSE 1

I feel the winds of God today
today my sail I lift,
though heavy oft with drenching spray
and torn with many a rift;
if hope but light the water's crest,
and Christ my bark will use,
I'll seek the seas at his behest,
and brave another cruise.

Jessie Adams, 1907
Voices United, 625

Every Canadian has a picture of the Bluenose—it's the one on the dime. The Bluenose was the fastest and most famous of the Grand Banks schooners—those fast sailing ships that rushed cod to port from the Grand Banks. But there were many others, among them the "James and Stanley." Recently I saw a painting of this schooner hanging in the home of the son of the man who was the skipper for 50 years. It reminded me of this hymn and I could imagine the sails "heavy oft with drenching spray and torn with many a rift." I thought of the dangers and hardships, the teamwork, the piloting skills, and the backbreaking labour that crew and skipper must have had. Many times they must have needed their faith in the Great Pilot. I hope the congregations of those little Methodist chapels in Newfoundland's coastal villages knew Jessie Adams' hymn; singing was important to them and a favourite hymn was "Eternal Father, strong to save" (*Voices United,* 659).

The fishermen on the Sea of Galilee had to face storms too. Though perhaps not of the ferocity of Atlantic storms, storms on that inland sea could be sudden and severe and perilous to those in small boats. Matthew describes in his gospel how the disciples were battling a headwind and rough sea as they attempted to cross to the other side. Jesus came to them, walking on the water, and called Peter to come to him. Peter started towards him, confidently walking on the water, but when he realized how strong the wind was, he was afraid and began to sink (Matt. 14:23–31). So long as his faith was strong, he was all right; it was fear that caused him to sink. Is there a message for us here?

In Matthew's story, wind represents danger. In this hymn, wind is a positive force; it is the wind of God, the wind that dries tears, brings comfort, courage, and the energy to continue the journey; the wind of God, the breath, the spirit, as the Greek and Hebrew words *pneuma* and *ruach* may be translated.

I first heard this hymn at a memorial service. The combination of words, music, and powerful singing made it a service of celebration. The mood was such that we could rejoice in the life we had gathered to remember while recognizing that we are all on our "onward way," ready to "brave another cruise" in this world or the next.

FOR PRAYER

God, our Creator, Redeemer, and Sustainer, may our imaginations enable us to appreciate the majesty and power of creation in our oceans, lakes, and rivers. And may we be carried forward by the winds of your Spirit. Amen.

2nd Sunday in Lent

TREE OF LIFE AND AWESOME MYSTERY (1)

Fran Ota

VERSE FOR THE SECOND SUNDAY OF LENT

In our call to be a blessing,
may we be a blessing true;
may we live and die confessing
Christ as Lord of all we do.

Marty Haugen, 1984
Voices United, 121

"The Lord your God turned the curse into a blessing for you, because the Lord your God loved you." (Deut. 23:5b) "The cup of blessing that we bless, is it not a sharing in the blood of Christ? The bread that we break, is it not a sharing in the body of Christ?" (1 Cor. 10:16)

As a child, I remember eating fish on Good Friday, and "giving up" something for Lent—yes, we still did that in the United Church—at least in our home we did, and most of my friends did too. I'm not sure I ever "gave up" anything, except maybe being a little less impulsive for a couple of weeks! What I liked about Lent so much was that we got to eat fish more than any other time of the year—fish being scarce and expensive in Winnipeg in the winter—and my mother would splurge and buy smoked Winnipeg goldeye, or make her wonderful "finnan haddie" with that fabulously fishy-salty cream sauce and boiled potatoes. I'm sure there is a rosy overcast to the lenses of this recollection, but there were times when I tucked into that creamy fish and felt truly blessed.

"Blessing" has many meanings—bestowal of favour, gift of God, well-wishing, consecration, sanctification, making happy or successful. So let's substitute some of these words in the Corinthians passage: "The cup of favour which we consecrate," the "cup of happiness which is a gift of God."

There is an old Christmas carol called "The trees of the forest"—the story of Christ's life and death told by the trees which went through his life with him as he grew up—the one which gave up its life to be a cradle for the baby, the one which gave up its life to be a table for Jesus and his companions to sit around as they ate, and the one which gave up its life for Jesus to be crucified on.

The trees of the forest gave up their lives to be a blessing to the one who came to bless. The tree on which Jesus was crucified also died, yet it became a tree of life. The disciples must have felt cursed as the events around them unfolded, yet the curse became a blessing. Each time we break bread and remember Jesus as we share the common cup, we have to remember that Jesus gave up his life, endured the curse of death, and turned the curse into a blessing, because of God's love for humanity. The blessing is still symbolized by that tree of life.

FOR PRAYER

God our Creator, we bless and thank you for the gift of life. In our call to be a gift, make us a true gift—don't let us fall into arrogance and pride at what a great gift we are. Help us to remember that to be "God's gift to the world" means that we must walk humbly with you. In this season of Lent help us to give up our pride in our accomplishments, our self-satisfaction in who we are, and turn the curse of our arrogance into a true blessing. Amen.

Monday

I'VE GOT PEACE LIKE A RIVER

Heather Hemming

I've got peace like a river,
I've got peace like a river,
I've got peace like a river,
in-a my soul.

African-American spiritual
Voices United, 577

A few miles north of my home flows the South Saskatchewan River. It actually originates in southern Alberta and rolls eastward, chiselling a path through this prairie land.

The water travels between parallel rows of river hills, the mottled green sentries standing shoulder to shoulder, silently watching as the river churns by. They watch the creeks negotiate mergers with the river, the places where the sediment swirls up like cream in a cup of coffee. They watch the river run on, leaving behind yesterday and flowing into tomorrow.

As the South Saskatchewan hurries past sandbars and brush, it smoothes away the coarse edges of the river bank and carves new paths where it can run freely. But this river doesn't just polish and erode—it also comes bearing gifts of rich soil, creating fertile plains like freshly spread tablecloths, places that will nurture seeds and support new growth.

Today's African-American spiritual celebrates peace like a river in the soul. The peace of God is a miraculous gift, especially when flowing through a tinder-dry soul that is tired of the pain and disappointments. The peace of God can smooth away the roughness sandblasted by anger and the splintered edges of dreams not realized. Cascading streams of peace can smooth the places where forgiveness has not been offered and heal the wounds that still seep.

Peace, like a river, can carve a new path through our soul, swirling freely and joyfully, bringing self-acceptance and contentment. Peace, like a river, can create fertile ground where God's seeds of renewed faith and trust may take root and flourish. The peace of God is a gentle, powerful gift.

Where do you need to feel God's peace flowing in your life? Drenching your parched spirit? Soothing you along your lenten journey with Jesus?

Where do you need to feel God's peace in your community? Washing away the acid words? Pushing through the thick silences?

Pray to God. Pray for peace in your soul. Pray for peace to flow through all of our souls. For when we know God's peace, we will find the courage to walk with Christ to Jerusalem.

FOR PRAYER
Our troubled earth, our troubled hearts, so long for your peace, O God. We long for it to wash over us, to fill us and renew us. Help us to open our hearts to you, that your peace would flow from us to others. May the mighty river of your love bring hope, courage, justice, dignity, and wholenesss to all. Amen.

Tuesday

TREE OF LIFE AND AWESOME MYSTERY (2)

Bernice Saulteaux

VERSE 1

Tree of life and awesome mystery,
in your death we are reborn,
though you die in all of history,
still you rise with every morn,
still you rise with every morn.

Marty Haugen, 1984
Voices United, 121

Lent is a time in which we come awaiting the tree of life and awesome mystery. This tree of life is the centre pole in our Medicine Lodge.

It is with great mystery that we see the tree used. It is the cross, where Christ was crucified for us. It is the centre pole of the lodge, that our Native people use for healing, praying, offering and spiritual name-giving.

Our Medicine Lodge people meet in the fall, winter, spring, and summer. They gather in different locations in Saskatchewan, Montana, and other places in the United States.

All people come wanting prayer and healing. They may be in mourning after losing a loved one in death. They may be suffering sickness due to an illness, drugs, or alcohol. They offer tobacco and cloth to the keeper of the lodge, who is a medicine man or woman.

During this four-day ceremony, 40 songs are sung each day. This reminds us of Jesus' 40 days in the wilderness.

After those seeking healing are prayed for, a feast is held to feed everyone who came. Our loved ones gone to the spirit world are also remembered. In closing, a dance is held. Our embraces are our farewell until we meet in the next singing time.

This is done three times a year. The fourth time, the tree of life is cut down by the spiritual men. The tree is used as the centre pole at the annual Medicine Lodge ceremony.

People from all over come to this ceremony. Individuals fast, dance, and offer sacrifices on behalf of others who come to find healing and new life. Native spiritual name-giving is also done at this ceremony.

This tree of life symbolizes the cross.

O tree of life, when Jesus was crucified upon you, his sacrifice for all people enabled a great healing force to be poured out upon our world.

This is the tree of great mystery. How did our ancestors before us know God's healing power? This was before Columbus and the missionaries came.

For Prayer

Creator God, as we prepare ourselves for the lenten season, we thank you for the great tree of life and awesome mystery. May we find forgiveness, healing, and grace, so that we can find new life. We thank you for all the saints gone on before us. They have left us the tree of life and awesome mystery to carry on. May the living waters of salvation flow in us and make us whole. Amen.

Wednesday

I Bind unto Myself Today

Donna Sinclair

Verse 3

I bind unto myself today
the virtues of the starlit heaven,
the glorious sun's lifegiving ray,
the whiteness of the moon at even,
the flashing of the lightning free,
the whirling wind's tempestuous shocks,
the stable earth, the deep salt sea,
around the old eternal rocks.

attributed to St. Patrick
Voices United, 317

People talk of paradigm shifts. I am lost. Once I cried for three days, a novice at the esoteric rites of e-mail without the proper password, the secret sign.

The fax machine has a mysterious line down the middle of the paper, the bottom element on the oven won't heat up and there is a mysterious, growing bubble in the bedroom ceiling where water is getting in and no one knows how or why.

There is a hole in the ozone.

I go, therefore, to St. Patrick. This is what it is to have ancestors in the faith. I will be rooted in tradition, stubborn in language, a pigheaded Celt in the face of change. I will bind to myself eternity, like Patrick, the virtues of the starlit heaven, the sun, the stable earth, the whiteness of the moon at even, the rocks, the deep salt sea. The strong name of the Trinity.

These things, nothing can change.

For Prayer

Give me courage, three-in-one and one-in-three, when my world quakes and shifts. In all and through all, you are my salvation.

Thursday

I Danced in the Morning

Ian MacLean

Verse 4

I danced on a Friday when the sky turned black;
it's hard to dance with the devil on your back;
they buried my body and they thought I'd gone,
but I am the dance and I still go on.

Refrain

Dance, then, wherever you may be;
I am the Lord of the dance, said he,
and I'll lead you all, wherever you may be,
and I'll lead you all in the dance, said he.

Sydney Carter, 1963
Voices United, 352

I tried every way I know how to help my mother warm to, if not come to love, "The Lord of the dance" but she wouldn't, couldn't, didn't. The song I mean—not the Lord. I know she's not alone. She was a woman who loved music, was ready to dance (she taught me a basic two-step before my first dance at school—in the daylight—when I was in grade eight), was full of fun and laughter, but church was no laughing matter and one didn't dance with Jesus! Pity.

I tried the trick of saying, think "life" whenever you come to that stumbling-block word "dance." It didn't work. It was one of those things about which we agreed to disagree. Oh, but what a reflection of Jesus' ministry this hymn is. He was a stumbling-block to so many good people. He just didn't fit the image of "anointed one." He didn't have what it takes to be the son of God. "If you are the son of God, come down from the cross and save yourself." He didn't. He couldn't. And the other miserable wretch hanging beside him said, "save yourself—and us!" If only he would save us! Who of us is ready to dance "on a Friday when the sky turned black?"

I find the Sydney Carter song hard to sing too. I find it hard to sing when it's sung to rhythm rather than words. How can the first verse be sung like the fourth verse? I think this is what my mother felt deep down—the incongruity of dance and death, of two-step to "they whipped and they stripped and they hung me high." But therein is the struggle. Sydney Carter is an intriguing and disturbing theologian, poet, songwriter, just as Jesus was country boy, carpenter, and correspondence-course rabbi. There is something mischievous and mysterious, teasing and tough, dizzy and depth-sounding in both of them.

As difficult as it seems, as it surely is, to "dance then, wherever you may be...I'll live in you, if you'll live in me," that remains the lenten invitation, the test of Holy Week, the trial of black Friday and the "joy through pain" Easter reality. The theme hymn (p. 1) in verse 2 says, "if we learn to live your story, we may die to rise anew." Now that my mother would understand. How about you? Can he have this dance?

FOR PRAYER

A thought: if you say "Yes," for heaven's sake, let him lead!

Friday

O GOD OF BETHEL

Judith Fetter

VERSE 3

Through each perplexing path of life
our wandering footsteps guide;
give us each day our daily bread,
and shelter fit provide.

Philip Doddridge, 1736
Voices United, 650

I had known Brazil would be different, but I had not expected to hate it. I had expected to be appalled by things I saw in the society—slums, malnourished children. I had not expected the church to be so different in its music and style of worship. Naively I had supposed that because they were our "partner" church, they would be like us.

I grew up in a beautiful old church which had a plaque on the wall with my great-grandfather's name on it: he had been its first minister. That church's special hymn, its "mission statement," if you will, was, "O God of Bethel," a hymn about a God who was dependable, who would be there in all our crises and who would lead us safely home.

So where was God in this very foreign place? I needed God desperately. God, I was told only half in jest, is a Brazilian and speaks Portuguese. I knew it was a joke but I was afraid all the same.

I found the God of Bethel one morning in the centre of the city. I had gone to the bank as usual to pay our rent, only to be told that something had changed and I had to go directly to the rental agency. That in itself was enough to make me anxious, but the worst thing was that I had only a hazy idea of where the agency was. Soon I was completely lost. I stopped at a news stand, but neither the vendor nor any of the passers-by could understand my Portuguese. I panicked, and to my embarrassment, began to cry. An old woman came over, said something I couldn't understand, put her hand on my arm and pointed. With nothing to lose, I went in that direction and within minutes was at the agency door.

So where was God in this foreign place? Did God only communicate in Portuguese here?

God communicated the way God always communicates: in surprising ways and through surprising people, this time a little old woman. The people of my childhood church had been right all along. God is a dependable God who is there in our crises, and who will indeed lead us home.

FOR PRAYER

Thank you, God, for being there through all the perplexing paths of life, and for helping us, in the midst of them, to grow. Amen.

Saturday

WILL YOUR ANCHOR HOLD

Ian MacLean

VERSE 1

Will your anchor hold in the storms of life?
When the clouds unfold their wings of strife,
when the strong tides lift and the cables strain,
will your anchor drift or firm remain?

REFRAIN

We have an anchor that keeps the soul
steadfast and sure while the billows roll,
fastened to the rock which cannot move,
grounded firm and deep in the Saviour's love!

Priscilla Jane Owens, 1882
Voices United, 675

I couldn't believe it! Is that true? It's back again in this new book! You mean I have a chance to repent and sing again "Will your anchor hold..." ? Is there nothing new under the sun?

I blush to confess there was a day when people heard me say "if I EVER sing that hymn again it will be too soon!" I think I got waterlogged. It was overkill. Or maybe I was too immature. Like the fresh young preacher of whom one weathered old parishioner said "he ain't old enough to have sinned enough to have repented enough to preach about it!" I'm glad it's back. This 60-year-old knows more than the sixteen-year-old did about "the storms of life, the straits of fear, the floods of death, and the gathering night." He also knows the terror of being adrift—at the mercy of currents of depression and waves of grief. Oh, for an anchor "grounded firm and deep in the Saviour's love."

This summer my son-in-law and I formed a "handshake" corporation and we bought a boat. Not a big boat, but it floats—in fact, it sails! Well, it has one sail, and on a good day two adults can enjoy the sun, sky, wind, and water and talk about life's mysteries (like, how do we get this thing upright again?) Most of the time I sailed alone—and I was astounded to hear me singing, "We have an anchor that keeps the soul...." Is that what the theme hymn for this lenten booklet (p. 1) means when it promises "every person lost and broken wears the body of our Lord"? He is anchor and anchorage. The one who travels with us and the one we return to. We are not spared the storms, the reefs, the breakers, nor will we cheat death. But in life, in death, in life beyond death, we are grounded firm and deep in the Saviour's love. I don't know if an inland, big city church can sing this hymn the way Maritimers can—but I can hardly wait. It will be a turn around for me—"repentance."

FOR PRAYER

A thought: knowing when to drop anchor takes wisdom; knowing when to weigh anchor takes courage; "Grant us wisdom, grant us courage for the living of these days."

3rd Sunday in Lent

COME AND FIND THE QUIET CENTRE

Don Parsons

Come and find the quiet centre
in the crowded life we lead,
find the room for hope to enter,
find the frame where we are freed:
clear the chaos and the clutter,
clear our eyes, that we can see
all the things that really matter,
be at peace, and simply be.

Shirley Erena Murray, 1989
Voices United, 374

How often the gospels show us a snapshot of Jesus, hiking off to a quiet place in the hills...to pray. On some occasions, he rose "a great while before day" to find that quiet centre. At other times, he took his long breath at the close of day. But whenever that occurred for him, we have the impression that such pause moments were essential if he was to function...and survive. Is it so for you, too?

The moment is mellow, and pure. You are enveloped by warm colour, like the layers of lavender light in the evening sky. You find yourself sitting on a log perhaps, or at the beach, or on your balcony or patio, waiting for that first star upon which you can hang your most earnest wish. The leaves around you are hushed and still. If there is any melody at all, it is the song of crickets in the grass, or the goodnight squawk of a gull floating in the updraft of evening air. The aroma is something like pine, or seaweed, or roses along the neighbour's fence. There is sanctuary in such sabbath moments. Some would call the experience "prayer"—this "quiet centre" that is often full of a communion that is more beautiful, more loving, and more holy than we know how to name.

Michael Tournier once described beauty as "the world's most widely distributed good." That insight serves as a powerful antidote to the notion that it is selfishness, greed, dishonesty, and power that is the true wealth of this world. Not so! Maybe it is something like beauty that is our world's most universal good.

Unfortunately, because of the congestion of our calendars, much of what is beautiful around us slips by unnoticed. There is something almost sinful about that. When we fail to notice the play of colours at eventide, the textures in a weaving, the progression of chords in a symphony or song, the play of light on a sleeping child, we have not just failed to catch a glimpse of something beautiful. We have lost touch with a God whose gifts are intended to sustain us in this "crowded life we lead." Beauty is the gift of a generous, loving God.

"Come and find the quiet centre in the crowded life we lead..." is an invitation once again to be still, and know God.

For Prayer

We pause, holy God.
We listen to the silence.
We know that it is not empty.
It is instead alive with your presence.
Help us to know that in this everyday moment...even here...we are on holy ground. Thank you.

Monday

You Never Saw Old Galilee

Bob Wallace

Verse 7

So, friends, although the sea be wide
and though your boat be small,
there's naught to fear
from time or tide;
the Master's Lord of all,
the Master's Lord of all.

Herman G. Stuempfle, Jr., 1989
Voices United, 673

Imagine those young sun-golden Galilean fishermen, Peter and Andrew, James and John, singing as they hand-tugged their heavy nets into the boats. Fishing was familiar. Faith was new. Jesus was wise enough to know this and to use their own language when he called them, "I will make you fishers of men."

This unusual new hymn blends the sacred and secular. The boisterous tune has overtones of a lusty, earthy life. At the same time, it is wedded to the mystery of God's presence and power. Here is incarnation in song, a rollicking union of flesh and spirit. Although the words are from the pen of an American Lutheran minister, the music is in the style of a British sea shanty. The song captures the conviction that marked the ministry of two noted eighteenth-century British church leaders—John and Charles

Wesley; namely, that daily work and deepest devotion belong together. The brothers were tossed out of their church for daring to bring the working day and worship of God into contact with one another. We take it for granted today, but there are still those who find it hard to see the presence of the divine in the rough and tumble of daily work. In each season of Lent, one area for prayerful examination is the degree to which we consciously search for ways to align our vocation with the will of God. It is a practice that is evident in the New Testament accounts of the young fishermen-disciples. It comes through strongly in this hymn.

At another level, this hymn has in it the sound of the sea. The sea is, for many, a powerful symbol of the vastness of God. The New England pilgrims would gather before worship on the shore of the ocean they had crossed to the New World. They would stand silent, at the margin of water and land, perhaps thinking of the old homeland beyond the horizon, but also taking in the breadth of God's creation and their own minuteness in God's presence. It is that spirit that produced a popular old prayer, often found on wall plaques, especially in the homes of fisher-folk. Make it your own today.

FOR PRAYER

Dear God, my boat is so small. Your sea is so vast. I rest on your mercy. Amen.

Tuesday

IN SUFFERING LOVE

Everett Hollis

VERSE 3

In love's deep womb our fears are held;
there God's rich tears are sown
and bring to birth, in hope newborn,
the strength to journey on.

Rob Johns, 1983
Voices United, 614

Our family of four were sitting in a restaurant beside the Trans-Canada Highway, in northern Ontario, shaken and shaking—inside and out.

Earlier that day we said the last of our goodbyes to family and friends and had set out for the Prairies and new lives in a far-distant place. We were feeling excited, yet hesitant, about moving to a pastoral charge in a town and area we'd never seen before. So, at midmorning, we set out in our two vehicles and began heading west.

Less than four hours into our journey, I watched in helpless horror as Ruth and Jennifer, travelling in the second vehicle, came within inches and milliseconds of being involved in a head-on collision with a truck that was towing a camper trailer.

We managed to get to the restaurant and now sat huddled in a booth engulfed in a sea of emotions, fighting the pull to turn back from our journey and to return to the comfort of familiar people and places. The pain, the fear, the losses, and the near losses seemed to wash over us and make the new land seem even farther away than before.

We had set out thinking, or telling ourselves, that this would be an adventure; we would camp along the way, see new sights, it would be enjoyable! But as the sea of feelings subsided, the anticipation was replaced by a sense of necessity and duty. We "had" to finish this journey.

As hunger in the wilderness had reminded the people of Israel of what they had left behind in Egypt, our brush with death reminded us of what we left and how much greater the losses could have been. Like our desert ancestors, we also deemed the cost too high and believed that there must be a better, easier, and safer way.

Like the Israelites of old, we finished the journey, and like them we encountered more difficulty as we travelled (there was another near head-on that same day). Looking back, I see that that journey is over, but my (and our) journey continues on.

As I sit at my desk and reflect on life since that trip I see again and again where I have wanted to leave my personal failures, conflicts, and life changes to return to the "comforts" of my personal Egypt. Each time, though, the strength and will to continue have come unexpectedly and have enabled me to continue on. Out of fear has come some courage, out of loss have come bits of hope, and out of darkness has come light.

FOR PRAYER

O God, you come to us in
unexpected ways.
You know our fears.
You hear our cries.
Your tears mingle with our own.
Help us to journey beyond our fears
with hope reborn.
May your strength and courage
be ours. Amen.

Wednesday

JESUS CAME, A CHILD LIKE ME

Don Parsons

VERSE 1

Jesus came, a child like me,
so the face of God I'd see,
God is not left far away,
God is with us every day.

REFRAIN

Live, Jesus, near us,
live, Jesus, with us,
live, Jesus, in us,
come, live in us today.

Walter Farquharson, 1987
Voices United, 583

It was the third Sunday of Advent. The children of our church school were lining up to enter the sanctuary for their Christmas concert. It was like a parade—wee angels with tinsel halos slipping off their heads; three regal Magi (all female—a fitting tribute, I thought, in this equal opportunity era); some barnyard animals whose familiar human faces smiled and winked at me; and many six- and seven-year-old shepherds in bathrobes and tea-towel headbands.

In order to be helpful, I was standing at the door, which I intended to hold open for them, as they made their way into the church. As we waited, one of those shepherds, a seven-year-old with deep brown eyes, looked up at me and very seriously said, "You can't be a shepherd, because you're not *young* enough!"

I will admit that he caught me off guard. Here was a child, explaining to the senior minister of the church, that "you can't be a shepherd (which is to say, 'you can't come to the manger'), because you're not young enough...." I wonder how many times my young friend had been told something like, "When you are older, you will be able to...," "When you grow up, you can...." Now he was saying to me, "When you become younger, you can...."

That moment was for me both startling and life-giving. Somehow an ancient Word was finding its way through all the years of history from the lips of one named Jesus, to the lips of a seven-year-old suburban shepherd, suggesting what it will take from me, to behold the mystery of the incarnation.

Perhaps that Advent insight can help to focus a lenten reflection, a healthy reminder that, unless we become like a child, we cannot enter the kingdom.

For Prayer

When my life becomes too complex, too sophisticated, put me in touch with the child within, so that once again in Jesus, a child like me, I can see your face, holy God. Amen.

Thursday

Maker of the Sun and Moon

Stephen Adams

Verse 1

Maker of the sun and moon, and
mother of the earth,
comes to life in human form to bless
all human birth:
Glory to God! Maker, Spirit, Son!
Giver and Gift, in love enfolded in One.

Peter Sharrocks, 1991
Voices United, 323

As a musician, I once had to provide music for a Jewish wedding, so I thought it wise to consult a Jewish friend. He was helpful with many suggestions. But finally, he said, all that's really important is to play "lots of happy music in a minor key."

Here is a hymn that celebrates the wonders of creation, nature, parenthood. These are experiences to celebrate, certainly. Jesus, too, was human, enjoyed friendship, wine, and a wedding celebration, presumably the music and dancing too, and he was aware that the lilies of the field are beautiful. But as we well know, human life begins in the pain of childbirth, and the human form ends in the certainty of death, and there's a story in the book of Genesis about Adam and Eve that tries to explain why this is so. (In this hymn I would prefer the phrase "mortal form," to "human form," I think: "Let all mortal flesh keep silence.") We profess our love of nature, we see it as the image of the Divine, and we are right in being outraged by our own greedy and ignorant desecration of the natural environment. And yet nature is not God: it is where mortal creatures live and die.

The sun and moon themselves are not eternal. They are aids to our poor imagination of what eternity might be like. It is only the Maker and Mother of all who comes with the true blessing of eternal life. Meanwhile, we are left to celebrate and rejoice in what we are given to know—the love of family and friends, the beauty and magnificence of nature and of human art—to celebrate them all with the happiest music we can muster, in a minor key.

For Prayer

Maker and Mother of all, we thank you for your gift of life, and the privilege of living in this beautiful world. We thank you for being the meaning in our lives. In response to your love, help us to live more fully in your praise, enjoying your gifts and returning them to those whose lives we touch. Amen.

Friday

Jesus, Keep Me Near the Cross

Ian MacLean

Verse 1

Jesus, keep me near the cross;
there a precious fountain,
free to all, a healing stream,
flows from Calvary's mountain.

Refrain

In the cross, in the cross, be my glory ever,
till my raptured soul shall find rest beyond the river.

Fanny J. Crosby, 1869
Voices United, 142

What is it the "old people" say? You don't miss the water till the well runs dry? Now I've said it so that puts me among the old people! That's okay. I'm feeling more comfortable with that.

"Near the cross, there a precious fountain...." Oh Fanny, we haven't sung words like that for 25 years in our church... "till my raptured soul shall find rest beyond the river." We hardly understand the language anymore. I close my eyes and in an instant see the faces and hear the voices of those who taught this hymn to me. The old people. My Baptist grandmother and Presbyterian grandfather. This hymn, like them, was dead years ago. And now here it is again—and so are they in my mind's eye.

But I didn't choose this hymn just for old times' sake. The theme hymn (p. 1), "Tree of life and awesome mystery" (that's how we talk—sing—now), offers verses for Lent. One of them, for the third Sunday, says "living water of salvation, be the fountain of each soul, springing up in new creation, flow in us and make us whole." Ah, the precious fountain is back again. It appears in other places too. Charles Wesley uses the image in "Jesus, lover of my soul." "Thou of life the fountain art, freely let me take of thee, spring thou up within my heart, rise to all eternity."

Many fountains are more for show than for slaking our thirst, just as many crosses are more for looking at than clinging to. But I daresay there are just as many trembling souls around as there were in your day, Fanny, as there were that day when Jesus, cross, and Calvary became one in fact and in faith's imagery. There was no precious fountain there. Just the blood, sweat, and tears of one who lived, "yea, though I walk through the valley of the shadow of death...." There was no healing stream flowing down that bald hill, just conscience-stricken tears. "Peter went out and wept bitterly...."

The "living water of salvation" is the river of remorse, the un-damming of a backlog of hurts, griefs, grudges, anger, fears, that must find outlet before the artesian well of God's goodness and grace can "flow in us and make us whole." Let's not deny ourselves this lenten possibility.

Ah Fanny, as one trembling soul to another, walking in the shadow of the cross, thanks.

For Prayer

A thought: the answer to a penny pincher's prayer—"free to all!" But remember, "freely have you received, freely give."

Saturday

Stay with Us through the Night

Donna Sinclair

Verse 1

Stay with us through the night.
Stay with us through the pain.
Stay with us, blessed stranger
till the morning breaks again.

Walter Farquharson, 1988
Voices United, 182

This is how it happens. The disciples meet the risen Jesus on the road to Emmaus. They are drawn to him, as we sometimes are to certain people, without recognizing him. They tell him about their grief over the loss of their friend, the one they had hoped "would set Israel free."

The conversation gives them comfort, and they press him to stay and have supper with them.

It's a simple story. This is what it is to be human, to find pleasure and comfort in simple things—walking, talking through troubles, sharing a meal, discovering a friend in a stranger.

But then there is this explosion, right in the middle of the narrative. Jesus breaks the bread and gives it to them, and immediately "their eyes were opened, and they recognized him."

We see Jesus just the same way, in the breaking of bread; a friend comes to the door with a drive-through coffee and doughnut. "Knew you were having a busy day," she says and vanishes. A small boy says grace before supper on a sticky August day: "Summer," he says happily, "is the nicest time of year." And a long-gone, much-missed daughter makes it home for Easter. The table is complete. And the risen Christ is there, as he is always there, in the circle at the food bank and at the premier's feast. Always.

For Prayer

Open our eyes, Lord. Let our sudden recognition of you be like a fire, burning in us. Amen.

4th Sunday in Lent

CHRIST BE OUR HOST

Bob Wallace

VERSE 1

Christ be our Host, welcoming, greeting:
this is the banquet your love has prepared!
Hear us we pray, entrance entreating,
this is the banquet your love has prepared!
Come to the table where mercies are spread!
Come to the feast, all who hunger.

Herman G. Stuempfle, Jr., 1994
Voices United, 465

There are countless images for God. One that is rarely noted, yet seems most appropriate, is God as "host." Picture a snowy winter evening. You have driven to a friend's home. Walking through an icy wind you approach the doorway, to have it open before you. The fragrance of fine dinner softens the night air. You can hear music and faintly hear the crackling fireplace. In the doorway stand host and hostess, arms stretched towards you in warm welcome. It seems a fitting image for our arrival at a communion service. David Johnson's lilting tune enhances the hymn's appeal.

Notice how the text has us "entrance entreating." The words hardly fit the scene we've laid out. They do, however, match our inner experience. We have the feeling that we must somehow entreat God's love. Inner peace is something for which we must strive. God's favour must be earned. All this runs counter to the biblical understanding of God. In a number of parables Jesus tells how God has prepared the table, but the guests are reluctant to come. There is no need to angle for an invitation to this banquet. This is the banquet love prepares. The host will be disappointed if we do not accept the invitation.

This lovely hymn is a gift from the Lutheran tradition which places a high value on the sacrament of Holy Communion. The tune began as an anniversary hymn for St. Olaf's College in Minnesota in 1964. The words to "Christ, be our host," were written for the tune later by Herman G. Stuempfle, President of a Lutheran seminary in Pennsylvania.

Throughout Lent, as we come to the table of the Lord, let the word with which our Roman Catholic friends are so familiar be a source of warmth to our spirits. In the broken bread and poured wine we meet the host.

FOR PRAYER

Christ, be our host, for this earth is your home, and we have come to know ourselves as welcome guests. Thanks.

Monday

In the Bulb There Is a Flower

Donna Sinclair

Verse 2

There's a song in every silence,
seeking word and melody;
there's a dawn in every darkness,
bringing hope to you and me.
From the past will come the future;
what it holds, a mystery,
unrevealed until its season,
something God alone can see.

Natalie Sleeth, 1986
Voices United, 703

It is all, I suppose, a matter of trust. Holding the baby after the birth. Rejoicing, wondering how to keep this small fragile one safe, how to teach these miniature fingers to be gentle and strong.

Planting the garden. Pulling apart the clumped perennials into dozens of new plants, abundant beauty trapped in tentative clusters of leaf and root, waiting. Wondering how such tender growth can make it through the January cold.

So we live, solemnly walking through our days. Oh, it could all go wrong—the seas could fill with tar, the soft air could lose its goodness. The trees could die.

But we can do nothing except raise our sons and daughters, plant our gardens, and trust the gospel, the long love story of our God who, laughing, reveals all in its season, all in God's own good and holy time.

For Prayer

We trust your hidden promise, God. Amen.

Tuesday

O HOLY SPIRIT, ROOT OF LIFE

Jessie McLeod

VERSE 3

O Holy Wisdom, soaring power,
encompass us with wings unfurled,
and carry us, encircling all,
above, below, and through the world.

Jean Janzen, 1991;
based on twelfth-century writings
by Hildegard of Bingen
Voices United, 379

Eight centuries have passed since Hildegard of Bingen, Abbess of the Benedictine convent of Rupertsberg near Bingen, on one of the most spectacular stretches of the river Rhine, wrote the poem on which this hymn is based. Hildegard was a remarkable woman: visionary, composer, poet, prophet, healer. She was a prolific writer. In addition to the ecstatic and mystical writings and music for which she is renowned today, she also wrote on such diverse subjects as, for example, medical science and the management of a Benedictine house. The rich metaphors of her writing—"the verdancy, the greening power of God," "the verdancy of God's justice"—often express her passionate love of creation. Such devotion to God's creation was not in keeping with her time or the theology of a church not noted for its concern for the natural world; eight centuries passed before her achievements as a woman and her love of creation were recognized as being consonant with the concerns of the late twentieth century.

We are indebted to contemporary theologians for discovering Hildegard's writings on the manifestations of Holy Spirit. We tend to think of the Holy Spirit only as the third person of the Trinity (as described in Acts II), but the words of this hymn remind us of other scriptural references as we look at each of the verses.

Verse 1: "Holy spirit...root of life, creator of all things" echoes the passage in Genesis 1:2, "the Spirit of God was moving over the face of the waters" (RSV); "a wind from God swept over the face of the waters" (NRSV). The Greek word *pneuma* and the Hebrew *ruach* can mean "wind," "air," or "breath." Hildegard's metaphor, "Lustrous movement of your wings...," suggests many references in scripture: "wings like a dove," "mount up with wings as eagles," "I bear you on eagle's wings," "wings of angels," "as a hen gathers her brood under her wing."

Verse 2: Though not named in this verse, the references are obviously to Jesus, who, according to Matthew, possessed the Spirit from conception. The angel appears to Joseph, saying "the child conceived in her is from the Holy Spirit," (Matt. 1:20); and again, at Jesus' baptism, "the Spirit of God descending like a dove." (Matt. 3:16) "Eternal vigour" denotes the energy and power of the Spirit which was from the beginning of time, and which Scripture reiterates as dwelling in Christ.

Verse 3: "Holy wisdom" is one of the gifts of the Spirit (I Cor. 12:8). In the Old Testament, wisdom is frequently referred to as feminine, as, for example, in Proverbs 8 and 9.

I have chosen the third verse of this hymn for the beginning of this commentary because it reinforces and gathers together the meaning of the whole. Its wonderful soaring quality gives us a sense of being lifted above the mundane and lovingly encompassed by God's Spirit. At the same time, the closing words remind us that the Spirit is with us as we journey through this world.

For Prayer

We give thanks, O God, for the varied gifts of your Spirit in our lives. Sharpen our awareness and appreciation of these gifts as we learn to recognize them throughout all of creation. Amen.

Wednesday

May The God Of Hope Go With Us

Judith Fetter

Refrain

Praying, let us work for peace,
singing, share our joy with all,
working for a world that's new,
faithful when we hear Christ's call.

Alvin Schutmaat, 1984
Voices United, 424

Hope is what we are most asked about by Canadians when we go to churches and talk about Brazil. "Is there any hope at all?" Canadians ask. "How did you keep from despairing in that place? How do they do it themselves?" It is easy to say how we stayed hopeful. We got our hope from them. How they do it is a good question.

I think the Portuguese language predisposes its speakers toward hope. The same word, *esperar*, means "to hope, to wait for, and to expect." "I hope (*esperar*) he will come today." "I am waiting for him (*esperar*) now." "I am expecting him (*esperar*) any time." The other word that Brazilian Christians have learned always to couple with hope is *luta*, which means "struggle." Philippine Christians have learned the same thing. "There is always hope," they say, "when you are part of the struggle."

Val is one of our lay preachers, a remarkable young husband and father whose life was transformed because a Christian minister believed in him. Val decided to use his own skills to set up a co-operative carpentry shop with his parishioners. They would make furniture, sell it, and share the profits jointly. "Is there sufficient market?" asked my cautious husband. "We think so," said Val. "Anyway we have to do something. Either we'll make it work or we'll all starve together. That's what ministry is, isn't it?"

Our little congregation once participated in a city-wide rally which kicked off a campaign to combat hunger. Many religious communities came to offer prayers, songs, dances, drumming, and to pledge themselves to work toward eliminating this terrible evil in their midst. Our people chose to sing a "Song of Victory," whose words expressed perfectly their hope and their commitment:

Want and hunger will there be?
NO!
Hate and violence will we see?
NO!
If we are faithful and continue
on the journey,
then the God who travels with
us will take all our pain away.

Think of those people, their brown faces shining with hope and joy, and renew your commitment using the words that follow.

For Prayer

Praying, let us work for peace,
singing, share our joy with all,
working for a world that's new,
faithful when we hear Christ's call.

Thursday

SHE COMES SAILING ON THE WIND

Bob Wallace

VERSE 5

Long after the deep darkness that fell upon the world,
after dawn returned in flame of rising sun,
the Spirit touched the earth again, again her wings unfurled,
bringing life in wind and fire as she flew on.

REFRAIN

She comes sailing on the wind,
her wings flashing in the sun;
on a journey just begun, she flies on.
And in the passage of her flight,
her song rings out through the night,
full of laughter; full of light, she flies on.

Gordon Light, 1985
Voices United, 380

In a review of a recent film, purportedly a feminist work, a reviewer stated, "This film is to feminism what Twinkies are to health foods." There is no danger of this popular Canadian hymn misfiring in its healthy feminist aim. While it celebrates the early life of Jesus from birth to baptism, its true theme is the work of the Holy Spirit. The jubilant refrain soars upward with, "She flies on!" Its author and composer Gordon Light, an executive in the national office of the Anglican Church of Canada, is a member of the Winnipeg-based singing group, the Common Cup Company, and this brilliant hymn, a virtual theme song, has gained them international recognition.

Inclusive language is a contentious issue in many churches. Our lenten devotions, in which we measure our own relationship to the faith, are bound to be affected by our position in this controversy. Throughout the ages the church has found ways to sing its faith. In this hymn Gordon Light helps us voice our confidence that confining God to a gender is to place human limitations on the divine. Surely God's person cannot be less than the personhood of all humanity. This assurance of the brooding, nurturing, life-giving nature of God breaks into melody, in laughter, in light and lightness. The heaviness of debate falls away and we are left with the lilt and lift of lyrics that celebrate the wondrous breadth of God's presence.

Nels Ferré, a noted theologian, was lecturing in Vancouver. Eager to communicate, he found himself coming to the end of his time in the final lecture. His pace accelerated till the words started to trip over one another. Ferré paused, laughed, picked up his notes, and said, "What a silly man I am. The Holy Spirit is the only teacher." If only we could recapture that genuinely humble spirit in our debates. Perhaps the prayer with which . Ferré concluded his lectures will help.

For Prayer

Come, Holy Spirit, come.
Come as the wind, and cleanse;
come as the light and reveal;
come as the fire and burn.
Convict. Convert. Consecrate.
Till we are wholly yours.
Come, Holy Spirit, come. Amen.

Friday

When Pain of the World

Judith Fetter

Verse 1

When pain of the world surrounds us
with darkness and despair,
when searching just confounds us
with false hopes everywhere,
when lives are starved for meaning
and destiny is bare,
we are called to follow Jesus and let
God's healing flow through us.

Jim Strathdee, 1976
Voices United, 598

Walking home from church one evening with four women, I congratulated one of them who had just brought home her seventh baby. "Daniel is actually my ninth," she told me. "Two of them died." All the other women told similar stories. I was the only one in the group who had never been to the cemetery with a tiny white box. A child dies every seven minutes in northeast Brazil of diseases directly related to poverty and malnutrition.

Eliabe was an ordinary four-year-old. I probably would not remember him if he had lived. He and his two-year-old brother, Elias, were inseparable and mischievous, often making nuisances of themselves during church services. One day Eliabe developed a high fever and within hours he was dead of meningitis. His family and the whole church grieved. Little Elias was desolate. Watching Elias made me realize how far from ordinary Eliabe had been. I did not know how special he was until I saw the huge hole he left in his brother's life.

A Canadian priest working the Amazon told us of the first time he was called to bury a baby. He tried, in stumbling Portuguese, to offer condolences and express sorrow, but he knew he was not getting through. Later one of the women caught up to him on his way home. "Padre," she said bluntly, "you need to start believing in your own gospel."

For six years it was our privilege to share the daily lives of people who live on the narrowest edge of survival. The last two verses of this hymn express something of what we learned from our courageous Brazilian neighbours: to trust; to be open; to take our fear, our guilt, our humble, stumbling courage, and offer them to God, who would somehow know how to use them. We learned that not knowing what to do didn't matter. We were called to follow Jesus, and let God's spirit flow through us.

For Prayer

The pain of the world always
surrounds us, loving God.
We don't want to hide from it,
but sometimes we can't bear it.
Forgive us. Renew us.
Keep us faithful. Amen.

Saturday

In Loving Partnership We Come

Jessie McLeod

Verse 4

Loving community we seek;
your hope and strength within us move.
The poor and rich, the strong and weak
are brought together in your love.

Jim Strathdee, 1982
Voices United, 603

My cousin recalls asking her father, a minister, why there were so many people in the church hard to get along with. Her father replied, "No other organization would have them." Church membership is not based on personal compatibility, but on the basis of faith in Jesus Christ. It is Christ who calls, not us, and consequently the community is sometimes formed by, as someone has said, "miserable, faltering sinners." Letters in the New Testament to the early church tell us that building and maintaining community was a major problem for many who responded to Christ's call. As an example, we read in Ephesians 4:2–3 a plea for unity "...bearing one another in love, making every effort to maintain the unity of the Spirit..." And further on, in verses 11–16, there is the variety of gifts given to members to "equip the saints for the work of ministry, for building up the body of Christ." A loving Christian community has always taken effort and commitment. And, as the verse above suggests, there is need to hold up the hope of the gospel while seeking divine strength.

The opening line of this hymn begins "In loving partnership we come...." The Oxford Dictionary defines partner as "sharer." We might well ask, where do we find partnering (sharing) within the United Church of Canada? Perhaps the place to begin is with an understanding of ministry. After years of attempts to define what we mean by "ministry," General Council accepted the following recommendation:

> Ministry is what God does in Jesus Christ, and all church members are called to share in that ministry. Some are called to Ordered Ministry (ordained to Word, sacrament, and pastoral care), or to Diaconal Ministry (commissioned to education, service, and pastoral care), others to lay ministry to be carried out in the workplace, the home, community, or wherever.

If we see ourselves as being in ministry, the need to work in partnership with one another is obvious.

"Partnering" is now the pattern of our work with overseas churches. At one time we sent missionaries out to mission fields who tended to be paternalistic, some bordering on arrogance. Now, only in response to specific requests from overseas churches, we send personnel who go as fraternal workers to work in partnership with the receiving church. In a further development, we now have a Mutuality in Mission program whereby overseas churches send personnel to us. These "missionaries" enrich and enlighten church life here in Canada.

"Partnering" is also the pattern of our work with Native Canadians. While the United Church has worked with Native people for many years, the relationship deepened when, at General Council in 1986, the Moderator, Rev. Robert Smith, delivered a formal Apology to Native peoples:

> We tried to make you be like us and in so doing we helped to destroy the vision that made you what you are....We ask you to forgive us and to walk together with us in the Spirit of Christ....

While the need for follow-up to the Apology continues, an All Native Circle Conference has been formed so that Native congregations can take care of their special needs, and their representatives have a voice in the courts of the church. Our first Native Moderator, Rev. Stan McKay, a Cree from Northern Manitoba, shared the gifts of his people regarding respect for creation, the importance of listening and consensus decision-making.

FOR PRAYER

Grant us, O God, sensitivity to those we exclude from our circle; courage to risk reaching out as we try to build a loving community; your grace to accept ourselves and one another. Amen.

5th Sunday in Lent

Let All Mortal Flesh Keep Silence

Stephen Adams

Verse 1

Let all mortal flesh keep silence,
and with awe and reverence stand;
ponder nothing earthly minded,
for with blessing in his hand,
Christ our God to us approacheth
our full homage to demand.

from the Liturgy of St. James,
trans. 1864
Voices United, 473

An acquaintance of mine once told me how much he enjoyed the astonishingly popular recording of Gregorian chant by the Spanish Benedictines of Santo Domingo. Knowing his musical taste usually ran to more raucous popular styles, I asked him what it was he liked so much. After some searching, he came out with it: "The music is so relaxing," he said. I nodded, but inwardly my mind fixed on centuries of monasticism, and I wondered how many of those who committed their lives to bare, cold cells did so in order to become "relaxed."

Relaxation implies a withdrawal from the world for refuelling, for recharging the batteries—in order to go back to it, unchanged. I wonder how often we treat Sundays this way? What this hymn portrays, however, with its haunting reminiscence of medieval chant, is something very different.

To "keep silence" in this sense implies a positive expectancy. Yet in our society, silence has negative connotations. Indeed, we do everything we can to avoid it. Where there is no noise of traffic or construction to assure us of our own usefulness, we lull ourselves with television, radio, even Muzak. We fear absence of sound as we fear absence of life. Contriving constant busy-ness, we cling to a sense of our own worth, and mask the unmeaning in our lives.

To find the positive silence, the awe and reverence, is to face the emptiness of self and to prepare a way for God. What God requires of us, according to theologian C.H. Dodd, is "an emptiness to be filled," an attitude in which we acknowledge our complete insufficiency and rely on the sufficiency of God. "It is to cease from all assertion of the self, even by way of effort after righteousness, and to make room for the divine initiative." In the hymn, we stand in silence: it is God who approaches us.

"Lord, make me an instrument of thy peace," said St. Francis in his great prayer. By waiting in silence, we may still learn to say with Jesus, "not my will but thine be done."

Monday

PRECIOUS LORD, TAKE MY HAND

Don Parsons

FOR PRAYER
God, we wait in silence with open hearts to feel your transforming presence. We feel empty and alone. Too often, in the preoccupations of crowded lives, in deadening habitual routine, in surrender to idleness, we cannot hear your voice. Yet like the still, small voice that spoke through the whirlwind, enter our hearts and minds so that we may live more fully in harmony with your will. Amen.

VERSE 1
Precious Lord, take my hand,
lead me on, let me stand,
I am tired, I am weak, I am worn;
through the storm, through the night,
lead me on to the light:
take my hand, precious Lord,
lead me home.

Thomas A. Dorsey, 1932
Voices United, 670

"We do not know how to pray as we ought, but the Spirit intercedes for us with sighs too deep for words." (Rom. 8:26)

I am encouraged when I glimpse here the apostle Paul on his knees, and overhear him confess that "we do not know how to pray..." In spite of the profound teaching of Jesus, and the careful formulae of the church's prayers, sometimes there are, for all of us, moments that feel like wilderness. The yearning lacks focus and direction, the centring-down feels empty and barren, and no prayer will come.

For a whole year Henri Nouwen, professor, writer, missionary, had wandered in a valley of spiritual despair, trying to sort out the meaning in his life. At Jean Vanier's invitation, he was spending the year at L'Arche in France, trying to discover how God would use the rest of his life.

In his journal, he describes how every day, whether he felt like it or not, he mustered the energy to go to L'Oratoire—the sanctuary space that is the heart of L'Arche. "Every time I enter L'Oratoire I feel a deep rest coming over me," he writes. "And even if it is hard for me to pray, I feel held there. It is as if the room prays for me. And if I cannot pray, I still go there so that I can at least breathe air that is rich with prayer."*

There are wilderness moments when "we do not know how to pray as we ought." But something keeps tugging us towards whatever is L'Oratoire (sanctuary space) for us. We keep at it, even when it feels so sterile and difficult. We keep at it when the words just won't come, and the yearning is nothing but a sigh. We keep at it, because we believe with Paul that those sighs are our most honest prayers.

Perhaps when what we are experiencing feels heavy and parched like wilderness, we need to place ourselves on some kind of holy ground. It could be that such a setting will offer us the gift of breathing air that is rich with prayer, and that this sanctuary space itself will pray on our behalf. Perhaps, in such moments, the Spirit will help us in our weakness, weaving our sighs into a tapestry of prayer through which God will take us by the hand, and lead us on...lead us home....

For Prayer

Sometimes, caring God, it is so difficult for us to clothe our yearnings with words, and the best we can do is be silent before you. In such moments, embrace us, hold us close, listen carefully to what is unshaped within us. For we dare to believe that such yearning is perhaps our most honest prayer. Amen.

**Nouwen, Henri. The Road to Daybreak. Doubleday: 1988, p. 28.*

Tuesday

The Love That Clothes Itself in Light

Jessie McLeod

Verse 3

Love, helpless, comes to Calvary,
rejected, scorned and crucified;
Love hangs in shame and dies alone;
but Love abased, is glorified.

Alan Gaunt, 1989
Voices United, 137

The opening line of this hymn directs us to Jesus on the cross: Love stands naked, betrayed, receiving blows. This scene reminds me of another, still to be seen today: the Plotzensee Memorial in Berlin. In this small, bare brick building resembling a backyard garage, hundreds of men and women were executed during the years 1933–1945, under Hitler's dictatorship. In this small room, eight metres by four and divided in half by a black curtain, the condemned were hanged not from gallows, but from meat hooks fixed in the ceiling. Those whom Hitler wanted to have a slow and agonizing death were hung by piano wire instead of rope. The building stands today as a memorial to those who had the courage to oppose the Nazi regime; among them were:

> *Adam Von Trott*, Rhodes scholar at Oxford, one of the group of army officers and intellectuals involved in the unsuccessful July 1944 plot to kill Hitler;
>
> *Johanna Kirchner*, who aided those wishing to escape from Germany; she wrote in her final letter, "I go my last way courageous and undaunted. Be cheerful and brave—a better future lies before you."
>
> *Julius Leber*, who worked to establish a new political order, wrote from prison: "One can terrorize the people by every possible means, but love can grow only out of humanity and justice.... For so good and just a cause the sacrifice of one's life is the appropriate price."

Not far from Plotzensee is the Church of the Atonement where, in the daily liturgy, the cry is voiced: "Who can save us from this hopeless predicament?" and the answer comes: "We thank God through our Lord Jesus Christ. He has accomplished it."

The first line of the second verse—"the Love that lifts the stars and sun..." contains images of divine power in creation like those in Isaiah 40:12–17, "Who has measured the waters in the hollow of his hand?" and Job 38:4–41, "Where were you when I laid the foundation of the earth?" To add a current image, today's newspaper has a photograph of the Andromeda Galaxy, through which, at 1072 million km per hour, it would take 10,000 years to travel from one end to the other.

This verse goes on: "Love...collapses, spent...goes on to death and total loss." What a contrast to the previous line! This is an illustration of the mystery of the cross of divine Love, spelled with a capital L, a mystery that continues to be as much a reality for us as for those whose eyes were fixed on the cross 2000 years ago.

Perhaps the best attempt of the early church to deal with this mystery is the hymn found in Philippians 2:5–11. Here is an understanding of the divine nature as manifested in Jesus' life, death, and resurrection. Here we learn that divine Love's way is through humility, service, sacrifice, and suffering. Tilden Edwards, in his book, *Living in the Presence,* suggests that humility leads to the pain of compassion and that, "It is the recognition of the mystery of the brokenness of the world that God meets with an open-armed cross rather than an army."*

The first line of the third verse may, on first reading, suggest that "helpless" means weakness. If, however, we believe that Love (God/Jesus) rejects the use of violent force when confronted with evil, the cross is not the result of helplessness, but rather it is the costly means Love chooses to overcome evil. The way of Love brings resurrection and the emergence of new life, as expressed in line 4, "Love abased, is glorified."

The Plotzensee Memorial is a reminder of an evil regime, a regime which was defeated and vilified, while the power of all those sacrificial deaths lives on forever.

FOR PRAYER

O Holy One, we pray that we may be able to recognize evil in its many guises in ourselves as in others; may the Love we see in Calvary heal our brokenness, leading from darkness into light. Amen.

**Edwards, Tilden. Living in the Presence. San Francisco: Harper & Row, 1987, p. 13.*

Wednesday

NEW EVERY MORNING

Ian MacLean

VERSE 4

The trivial round, the common task,
will furnish all we ought to ask,
room to deny ourselves,
a road to bring us daily nearer God.

John Keble, 1822
Voices United, 405

The first verse of the theme hymn for this lenten booklet (p. 1), which may be a new one to you as it is to me, ends declaring, "still you rise with every morn...still you rise with every morn." Like it's just too good to be true!

It reminds me of a hymn I have known and loved from the fading memory of childhood. In the *Hymnary* it was #530; in the *Hymn Book*, #360, and in *Voices United,* #405. "New every morning is the love...." Like the grace of God, it's there before I open my eyes. In fact, it opens my eyes! My only challenge is to see. Aye, there's the rub.

Just as we need the season of Lent in the church year, we need lenten times in every day. The hymn says, "room to deny ourselves...." What an interesting phrase to turn over in one's mind. Even the time taken to do that accomplishes something of the purpose of the poem. "Room" suggests space—you can furnish it in your own way. How large is it? Does it have windows? Is the door open or closed? What does it smell like in there? Is it cosy or cold? Are you furnishing your room? Room suggests space. Room also suggests time. Can we find any elbow room in busy schedules? Are we ready to deny the demands of daily agendas enough to review the roads we're on and ask if any of them are "bringing us daily nearer God"?

And what does that mean if not to see the sacred in the secular; the burning bush in the business of our day? As Abraham Heschel says, "the road to the sacred leads through the secular."* The trivial round, the common task, "will furnish everything." A retreat can be helpful. Holy places are important. But the "room to deny yourself," which is the place where you cherish and nurture your ability to hear the "still small voice," becomes the holy of holies each day. When summer comes, I hear it in the Salutation of the Dawn. If you're an old church camper you will have heard it too.

> Listen to the salutation of the dawn.
> Look to this day, for it is life,
> the very life of life....

New every morning—this very morning—is the love, is the room, the space, the road and the one who, rising early, says, "follow me." Just do it.

For Prayer

A thought: be still, breathe deeply and say quietly, "love as near as every breath."

**Heschel, Abraham. I Asked For Wonder. Crossroad Publishing: 1984, p. 57.*

Thursday

Now the Silence, Now the Peace

Mac Watts

Now the silence Now the peace
Now the empty hands uplifted
Now the kneeling Now the plea
Now the Father's arms in welcome
Now the hearing Now the power
Now the vessel brimmed for pouring
Now the body Now the blood
Now the joyful celebration
Now the wedding Now the songs
Now the heart forgiven leaping
Now the Spirit's visitation
Now the Son's epiphany
Now the Father's blessing
Now Now Now.

Jaroslav J. Vajda, 1968
Voices United, 475

The age of the universe is calculated not in hundreds or in thousands of years, not even in millions, but in billions. The time span is so great we can have no real sense of it. And those calculations also relate to the size of the universe, for scientists are noting the number of billions of years it takes light to travel from some of the stars to us. It is unimaginably old light which has travelled unimaginably great distances to touch the eyes of people living on "a second-rate planet revolving around a tenth-rate sun" (Reinhold Niebuhr). We can make the question of the psalmist our own without a doubt: "What are human beings that you are mindful of them, mortals that you care for them?" (Ps. 8:4)

This verse in *Voices United* by Vajda, however, reflects the gospel concern about this moment. We are not lost in the immensity of time, but are found and touched by God in specific occasions. "Now is the acceptable time; see, now is the day of salvation!" (II Cor. 6:2) "At the right time Christ died for the ungodly." (Rom. 5:6) God's relationship with us is not so much timeless as it is timely. The present moment is precious to God because every moment for us is a turning point. When any of us looks back on our personal history, we are amazed at the "coincidences" that changed the course of our lives.

A friend of mine got up one morning, turned on the radio, and heard the announcer read the biblical text to be used in the next song on the program, and in that moment decided she must go to church somewhere, though she had never in her life been part of the church. She has never stopped going. And we can also recognize the negative side of some turning points in our lives. Think of sentences like, "If only I hadn't been in such a hurry, she would be alive today."

Our relationship with God is to be found in these untidy, insecure, sometimes tragic moments. In fact, an essential part of Christian faith is trust in the providence of God. At one level everything is subject to the wayward, the utterly unpredictable, conditions of existence. We could say that everything is out of "control." But we remember that God made a promise to Israel that the Messiah would come, and though everything militated against trust in such a promise, some held on to it.

Centuries passed without fulfilment, and then one day a Jewish girl was visited by a messenger who said that of her the Saviour would be born. It was Now that she had to give her response, one way or the other, and she gave it. Some years later Jesus approached some fishermen and said, "Follow me." It was Now that they had to give their response, one way or the other, and they gave it. In Gethsemane, Jesus said to Judas, "Friend, do what you are here to do." It was Now that he had to give his response, one way or the other, and he gave it. A few years later the risen Jesus addressed a zealous follower of the covenant, "Saul, Saul, why do you persecute me?" It was Now that a reply had to be given, and he gave it.

Now the Spirit's visitation
Now the Son's epiphany
Now the Father's blessing
Now Now Now!

For Prayer

Eternal Light, shine into our hearts; eternal Goodness, deliver us from evil; eternal Power, be our support; eternal Wisdom, scatter the darkness of our ignorance; eternal Pity, have mercy upon us; that with heart and mind and soul and strength we may now seek your face, and at the last be brought by your infinite mercy to the holy presence, through Jesus Christ our Saviour. Amen. (Alcuin)

Friday

Now the Green Blade Rises

Donna Sinclair

Verse 1

Now the green blade rises from the buried grain,
wheat that in dark earth many days has lain;
love lives again, that with the dead has been:
love is come again, like wheat arising green.

John M.C. Crum, 1928
Voices United, 186

To be a gardener is to believe that out of dark earth will come amazing green.

It is to feel in your bones the story of Demeter and Persephone—remember the lovely young Persephone stolen away to Hades by the god of the underworld? Remember her mother Demeter, goddess of all that is fertile and rich, keening in anguish, sending the whole world into winter to share her pain?

And then, months later, Persephone is returned, matured by her sojourn in the underworld, a woman.

This story endures because it is our own. All of us know the descent into grief and darkness, the slow underground maturing of our faith—and the return, older, wiser, wounded, stronger, into light. It's the story of Jesus, nurtured by the quiet tomb into a god, or—as Mary thought—a gardener.

We gardeners know these stories. And we wait.

FOR PRAYER

Ah, but we worship you, Deity of the fertile earth. Love is come again, like wheat arising green.

Saturday

THOUGH ANCIENT WALLS

Bob Wallace

VERSE 1

Though ancient walls may still stand proud
and racial strife be fact,
though boundaries may be lines of hate,
proclaim God's saving act!

REFRAIN

Walls that divide are broken down;
Christ is our unity!
Chains that enslave are thrown aside;
Christ is our liberty!

Walter Farquharson, 1974
Voices United, 691

In 1983 the churches of Canada hosted the sixth Assembly of the World Council of Churches in Vancouver. The theme was, "Jesus Christ, the Life of the World." Poets and musicians from around the world submitted new hymns on the theme. While each honoured Jesus Christ, the recurring refrain was the need for unity in a broken world, the need to put an end to the death of community. One of the finest hymns submitted came from Walter Farquharson of Saskatchewan, who later became a most approachable Moderator of the United Church. Walter has spent his life in a vibrant rural ministry and his many hymns carry the flavour of his prairie home. This one is universal in its call to break down all walls of separation. The words have great power, with something of the rugged strength of the Canadian west. Ron Klusmeier's music carries the note of surging hope.

Lent is a time of self-searching and self-assessment. Lent is also a season of confession. I recall many years ago flying over Africa and being stunned when the pilot walked into the passenger compartment and I saw that he was black. My mind told me that his skin pigment was totally unrelated to his competence as a pilot but my heart, for the moment, was unconvinced. Years of conditioning could not be banished in a moment of rational reflection.

Now, of course, years of a more sane approach have changed all that. Yet I wonder if some males might still have the same response to the presence of a female aircraft pilot! Long reflection on the incident helped me to see how we assign others a place that boxes them in. Racism, sexism, ageism all have to do with pigeon-holing people, making judgements about where they belong that are just as divisive as the old Jim Crowism that assigned one set of bus seats to blacks and another to whites.

This Lent ask yourself how often your heart and mind create such walls that divide. The hymn helps us to see the need to break down the walls that separate us.

For Prayer

God of our mind, God of our hearts,
break down the walls that separate
us and unite us in a single body.
Amen.

Palm/Passion Sunday

WE MEET YOU, O CHRIST

Judith Fetter

VERSE 4

You choose to be made at one with the earth;
the dark of the grave prepares for your birth.
Your death is your rising, creative your word;
the tree springs to life and our hope is restored.

Fred Kaan, 1966
Voices United, 183

Antonio's father owned a sugar plantation. Antonio knew it would one day be his, so he went to university to study agriculture. But while he was there his plans changed. He became a Christian, and suddenly became aware of the exploitation and oppression of the workers in his family's cane fields. His early efforts to make changes succeeded only in driving a wedge between him and his father, who finally disowned his son. Antonio left agriculture and enrolled in the Methodist Seminary. He met and married beautiful Celia, and they had a son whom they named Roberto after his grandfather.

Newly-ordained Antonio, with Celia, Roberto, and baby Rebecca, came to a tiny fishing village on the northeast coast of Brazil. Slowly they learned to cope with the deprivations of that place: the shortage of food and drinkable water; the fact that medical care was many hours away over terrible roads. They were better off than many of their parishioners, for Antonio at least had a salary and could buy what food there was. Many of the local people were so poorly paid by the boat and land owners that they could not buy the fish they risked their lives to catch, nor the beans and corn they laboured long hours to grow.

One day Antonio was at dockside visiting with his flock. "Why don't you fishers form a union?" he asked, remembering the sugar cane workers. That Sunday two pistol-packing men came into the church. "Pastor," they said, as all the people listened, "you stay away from the docks, or your babies will grow up without a father."

Antonio and Celia stayed another year in that village. Antonio did not mention unions, but he did preach regularly about justice, dignity, and liberation as the marks of the gospel of Christ. At the end of the year the bishop moved them, because the threats to Antonio's life were increasing.

"You choose to be made at one with the earth," says the hymn. As the choice was there for Christ, so it is there for each of us. When we choose to identify with the exploited and oppressed, we come into conflict with the oppressors, come face to face with "the dark of the grave." It takes great courage, sometimes, to believe that the darkness is preparing us and our society for new birth.

In your meditation today, put today's hymn together with these beautiful Brazilian words.

For Prayer

If the seed does not die when it falls
to the soil, there will be no glad
harvest to honour our toil. If the
seed gives its life for the life of the
bread, then joy and communion will
rise from the dead. Amen and amen.

Monday

Forgive Our Sins, as We Forgive

Mac Watts

Verse 2

How can your pardon reach and bless
the unforgiving heart
that broods on wrongs,
and will not let
old bitterness depart?

Rosamond E. Herklots, 1966
Voices United, 364

In our normal church discourse there is nothing that we speak more easily about, it might even be said, more glibly about, than God's forgiveness. The reality of that forgiveness, our desire for it, and our readiness to receive it, are all taken for granted. In this fine hymn, "Forgive Our Sins as We Forgive," Rosamond Herklots recognizes that it is a process with more than one level; part of it involves our relationships with one another. In fact the springboard for her hymn is to be found in the words of Jesus spoken on the occasion when he provided a model prayer for his disciples. He says that they might pray like this: "Our Father, who art in heaven..." and at the conclusion he adds: "For if you forgive others their trespasses, your heavenly Father will also forgive you; but if you do not forgive others, neither will your Father forgive your trespasses." (Matt. 6:14)

Very tough words. It seems that there is an unalterable condition tied to God's forgiveness; we don't receive it unless we have forgiven others. But since we talk rather glibly about forgiving each other, it must be a fairly easy thing to do. This, alas, is not the case. With a few minutes' thought, pastors who read these words will be able to recall instances of weddings and funerals involving family members who hadn't spoken to one another for years. They will be able to think of marriage counselling sessions where husband and wife, fine people both of them, had unresolved grievances with their partner that went back years. But all of us, even if we remain unaware of the foul pond of anger and resentment within ourselves, do not have to go far in our conversations with others before picking up signs from them of a closed heart toward this person or that over some perceived problem. And it is depressing to note how often the problem, to an outsider, seems to be a trifling one.

Perhaps during this lenten season we might find someone with whom we can explore the unresolved angers and resentments we have been carrying, getting them out into the open. This can be a process of putting them behind us and forming a forgiving heart toward those that have hurt us. It is always difficult, sometimes enormously difficult, to do this, and yet this is the means in which we find, not only forgiveness between ourselves, but the forgiveness of God. It's not that God is holding back on forgiveness until we forgive others, but that we aren't ready to be reconciled to God while our hearts remain hardened against another.

O cleanse the depths within our souls
and bid resentment cease;
then, bound to all in bonds of love,
our lives will spread your peace.
(Verse 4)

For Prayer

Almighty God, Spirit of purity and grace, in asking your forgiveness I cannot claim a right to be forgiven, but only cast myself upon your unbounded love. I can plead no merit or desert; I can plead no extenuating circumstance; I cannot plead the frailty of my nature; I cannot plead to the force of the temptations I encounter; I cannot plead the persuasions of others who led me astray; I can only say, for the sake of Jesus Christ your Son, my Lord. Amen.*

**Baillie, John. Diary of Private Prayer. Oxford: 1966, p. 79.*

Tuesday

When Jesus Wept

Stephen Adams

When Jesus wept, the falling tear
in mercy flowed beyond all bound;
when Jesus groaned, a trembling fear
seized all the guilty world around.

William Billings, 1770
Voices United, 146

When I was little, the Baptist girl who lived next door used to quiz me about the Bible—why, I don't know, because I never knew the answers. "What's the shortest verse in the Bible?" she demanded. "Jesus wept."

That stuck in my mind, and the terse phrase still startles when I encounter it in the story of Lazarus, as told by John. It is not hard to understand Jesus weeping for the death of a friend, nor is it hard to understand that his weeping should lead him to an act of mercy. But the act itself—raising Lazarus from the dead—is a mystery surpassed only by Jesus' words at the time: "I am the resurrection and the life."

William Billings' compact verse draws attention to the parallel between Jesus' tears for Lazarus and his groans at his own crucifixion. But he gives this one more paradoxical twist: if Jesus' tears evoke mercy, why should his groans arouse a "trembling fear"?

The "guilty world" can hardly expect to deserve mercy, of course; but I wonder if this fear of being condemned is not surpassed by the utter terror of being forgiven. Coming alive again is a wrenching experience. It means living in full awareness of our reliance upon God; and it means dedicating a renewed life in the world to what Dietrich Bonhoeffer called, memorably, "the cost of discipleship."

What is the shortest hymn in the hymn book? I'm not sure, but with its single verse it may well be this one. Yet William Billings' wonderful melody for his own verse is special: it is a musical canon, a "round." Like "Row, row, row your boat," once it gets started, it can keep on going forever. The shortest hymn in the book is also the longest. The tears, the groans—and the forgiveness and the salvation—are happening all the time. They do not end until the end.

For Prayer

Almighty and eternal God, we feel the presence of your love—a suffering love, a forgiving love, a redeeming love—that in joy or dejection continues to uphold us. Such love is mysterious to us because we see it in the mirror of our own lovelessness. Help us to be more receptive, so that your love may flow through us and touch the lives of those around us, at home and in our community. Amen.

Wednesday

LORD OF ALL LOVE

Don Parsons

VERSE 1

Lord of all love, all life, and death,
giver of time and place and breath,
hear us as now we bring our loss
into the presence of your cross.

VERSE 2

Sing us the songs we cannot sing,
pardon the praise we cannot bring,
speak all the words we cannot say,
pray for us, Lord, we humbly pray.

Colin Gibson, 1987
Voices United, 495

The teenagers, I noticed, gathered in small clusters, their blank stares betraying their shock and grief. They sought solace in the hugs they liberally shared with each other. Some clutched flowers, others held baseball caps which they intended to leave with the casket. Honest tears made wet lines on the cheeks of guys and girls alike. On this sunny Saturday in June, these teens, many for the first time, were facing the reality of death. Three days earlier, four of their peers had been killed in a car accident.

I had been asked to conduct two of the four funerals that day. The sense of inadequacy was almost overwhelming. Many in those sorrowing congregations that morning would have had some familiarity with the biblical imagery of hope and comfort, but most, I suspect, did not. How does one then, in a very few minutes, begin to build a spiritual scaffold that might give grieving folk some support? How can one speak of Easter faith to teens and others for whom the church and its spiritual perspectives about life and death is largely foreign territory?

The trauma of that week, in a dramatic, tragic way, reinforced for me how vital it is to be exposed to spiritual truth. As a parent, I want our children, through the nourishment of worship and their involvement in the lives of other "searchers" in and around the church, to have the opportunity to own for themselves the treasure of faith and love that comes alive in the motley family that is our congregation. Why? So that even if they move for awhile beyond the structure of the church, they will at least have some faith handles to hold onto when life's crises crash in upon them.

I know that an experience of church can never inoculate us against life's traumas. Sorrow still sears even the hearts of the faithful. But there is something in me that wants to believe that faith, no matter how fragile, does make a difference. It helps us to understand, however inadequately, that "in life, in death, in life beyond death, God is with us, we are not alone!" Thanks be to God!

For Prayer
That darkest mystery is here;
sorrow and pity, anger, fear;
conquer once more, dear Lord,
death's sting; faith, trust, and
consolation bring. (Verse 3)

Maundy Thursday

Jesu, Jesu, Fill Us with Your Love

Judith Fetter

Verse 1
Kneels at the feet of his friends,
silently washes their feet,
master who acts as a slave to them.

Refrain
Jesu, Jesu, fill us with your love,
show us how to serve
the neighbours we have from you.

Tom Colvin, 1969
Voices United, 593

We held several foot-washing services in Brazil, sitting in a circle, each person in turn both receiving and giving. Usually we washed only one foot, but I remember one beautiful old man who enjoyed it so much he put his other foot into the basin before I got up from my knees.

In another circle, my husband, Lawrie, moved the basin in front of Tarquinio and knelt down. It was a group of Methodist lay preachers who came together regularly for training and fellowship, men from the villages, poor, semi-literate, deeply committed. Tarquinio was new in the group and when he saw the white, foreign pastor kneeling at his feet he was horrified. "Oh no, Pastor," he breathed, and drew his feet as far under his chair as he could. Lawrie waited a few moments, silently pleading, then quietly moved to the next person.

The bishop was upset. "How will we ever end racism," he cried, "if we blacks cannot accept the whites when they come to us on their knees?" We were sad but not really surprised. "Jesu, Jesu," we prayed, "show us how to serve these neighbours we have from you."

José and Zeza formed a team with us to purchase equipment for our new day-care centre. I think they included us partly out of courtesy, but mostly because we had a car! On our first shopping expedition, lunch time found us far from the centre but close to our apartment, so I invited them for soup and muffins. José was sure he should not sit at the table with us, but with Zeza's help we convinced him, and afterward he told us his story. As a young man he had worked at an American Services Base, which was then on the Brazilian coast, as a personal servant to the officers. "They were friendly," he said. "We did a lot of things together. But never could I eat with them at their table. I wasn't good enough for that."

There is a Brazilian song that imagines the coming reign of God. "How will it be on that day?" the song wonders, and this is its answer: on that day black people, aboriginals, those of mixed blood, and whites will all eat together at the same table.

For Prayer

We want to serve our neighbours, Jesu, to kneel at their feet, ask for and receive their forgiveness. Help us to live with their pain, and our own. Amen.

Good Friday

THE LOVE THAT CLOTHES ITSELF IN LIGHT

Don Parsons

VERSE 5

Though Love is lost, Love finds us here;
though Love is absent, Love remains;
where Love is finished, Love begins;
where Love is dead, Love lives and reigns!

Alan Gaunt, 1989
Voices United, 137

...THUD...
...THUD...
...THUD...

Three crosses planted in mother earth
three bodies suspended in stony silence
three forms growing limp under a boiling sky
...execution...
such a grotesque spectacle, their dying
the indignity is public, etched forever on history's memory
the cries wrench out of the soul's deep abyss
shivering cold the hearts of the curious.
"It is finished! Into your hands, God, I commend my spirit..."
the day after sabbath dawns as innocently as any other
the sun first peeks, then explodes over the eastern edge of earth
the horizon is clean—no dark beams mar its beauty this day
garden fragrance hangs warm in the soft dawn
the earth yawns awake, dancing with diamonds of dew
to the garden-tomb they pilgrim with spices
one final gracious act for this teacher they love
"Do not be afraid...He is risen as he said..."
...remember...
"I will not leave you desolate...
Peace is my gift to you..."
"though Love is lost, Love finds us here..."
Love is absent, and remains; finished and begins...
Love, though dead, both lives and reigns...
"Mary"
and we know.

FOR PRAYER

Crucified Saviour, naked God,
you hang disgraced and powerless.
Grieving, we dare to hope,
as we wait at the cross
with your mother and your friend.
(*Voices United,* 140)

Holy Saturday

As We Walked Home at Close of Day

Fran Ota

Verse 3

We sat to eat our simple spread,
then watched the stranger take the bread;
and, as he said the blessing prayer,
we knew that someone else was there.

The Iona Community, 1988
Voices United, 184

"Then their eyes were opened, and they recognized him...." (Luke 24:31)

Earlier this year I had a delightful experience, sitting in the car with a friend, in the dark, late at night outside a doughnut shop, eating doughnuts and laughing our faces off. It was also a profound experience of recognition, each of us knowing something about the other that we had not known before, and yet somehow *had* known.

The moment of recognition—what is that moment? What happens?

You look into someone's eyes and recognize there someone you know, someone you care for, someone you have missed. Sometimes it happens when you have known that person only a short time; sometimes you know someone over again in that moment.

The word recognition really has two parts: "re" and "cognition," the "knowing again." Those moments of recognition fill holes in your life, find the places that were empty, or dry and thirsty; they feed those parts of your soul that needed feeding. Sometimes someone reaches your soul when you are not even aware of the need, until that moment of recognition happens.

Jesus and the disciples went to Jerusalem to celebrate the Passover. After his death, the disciples fled Jerusalem, certain that life had fallen apart; they descended into the depths of despair. In the resurrection Jesus began a new life; in the simple gesture of blessing and breaking bread at table, he was known; and the disciples, although they were not aware of it then, also began a new life.

In the knowing of Jesus at table, a new Passover was created—a celebration of release from spiritual bondage. The word again became alive and was known.

In that simple gesture—breaking of bread and celebrating at the community table—Christ is known to us. In that simple gesture—breaking bread and sharing around our home tables, or eating doughnuts with a friend late at night and laughing—we are known to each other and Christ is known to us.

For Prayer
O God, it is you who gives us our daily bread, so that we may have the experience of breaking it with friends, and knowing Jesus face to face. Each day you give us is a small Emmaus road, in which each person with whom we share life is the face of Jesus, with whom we share the grace of life after death. Help us to be open to those moments of recognition; help us to learn from them and make the most of them. Amen.

Easter Sunday

Midnight Sharpness, Starfields, Fading

Fran Ota

Verse 1
Midnight sharpness, starfields, fading,
creeping hues engulf the east,
strips of gravecloth cloud reflecting
faintest lines in crimson-grey;
herald Dawn's first heartbeat glowing,
blood-red streaks of fire flow
'cross the fields of furrowed labour,
signs of living, promise, hope.
Neil Lemke, 1990
Voices United, 181

"Yours is the day, yours also the night; you established the luminaries and the sun." (Ps. 74:16) "The one who sows the good seed is the Son of Man; the field is the world, and the good seed are the children of the kingdom." (Matt. 13:37–38)

Just outside Tampere in Finland there is a beach called Rauhaniemi. If you walk a little distance from the sauna along the lakeshore, you will find a small outcropping of rock right on the water where you can sit all night and watch the sunset—and the sunrise—at the same time, east and west touching shoulders with each other so far north. To the west, pale pinks and yellows streak the sky, casting a gentle gold outline on the grey cloud, and reflecting on the lake's surface, crystalline, quiet, the loon's mournful call emphasizing the stillness and silence. To the east, a burnished red-gold lacing edges the same clouds, streaks of orange and yellow flare up, flaming the sky and setting the surface of the lake alight.

Without the crucifixion of Christ, there would have been no Easter joy. With the death of Christ, it seemed that light had gone out of the world. The disciples were lost in despair, their hopes dashed at the foot of the cross. Yet, without the darkness of that day we call Good Friday, without the terror which took hold of the disciples, there would have been no Easter dawn at all, and the women at the tomb would have had no good news. Side by side with the sunrise, there is also the sunset. The day belongs to God, but so also does the night.

How lucky we are that we don't have to live those events that the disciples did—how lucky we are that we know Easter comes. We have become blasé, too secure—the tragedy and the enormity of those events have faded into little more than routine religious observation.

God loved creation so much that Jesus was freely given, even to death. The God who never gives up on human beings took the radical step of becoming human, and lived and died as a human. The seed was planted as frail flesh, but it rose to become a new and glorious flower, with the power to transform all the other mundane seeds. Across the furrowed fields of God's labour, the first warming rays of that wonderful sunrise cause new life to begin; the little mundane seeds rise, and blossom into glorious flowers, signs of hope and promise. God's fields become God's garden, flaming with God's rainbow of colours in the bright sunshine.

For Prayer

O God, loving and creative farmer, we lie here, little seeds in our furrows, hoping somehow the rays will pass over us, yet yearning for the warmth which will grow us into something new and beautiful. The transformation frightens us, that chill which comes with the sunset. The light is so bright we cannot look, yet its warmth draws us constantly in its direction. It flames in our hearts till the flower must burst out, and sing with all creation in the Easter garden, "Alleluia! Alleluia!"

Acknowledgements

82 © 1992 Borealis Music.

107 © 1994 Selah Publishing Co. All rights reserved. Used by permission.

109 © 1964 Oxford University Press, Walton Street, Oxford OX2 6DP, England.

113 © 1992 Borealis Music.

119 © 1972 Westminster John Knox Press.

121 © 1984 G.I.A. Publications, Inc.

137 © 1991 Stainer & Bell Ltd. All rights reserved. Used by permission of Hope Publishing Company.

181 © 1990 Neil Lemke, 11512 43rd Ave., Edmonton, AB T6J 0Y5.

182 © 1986 Walter Farquharson.

183 © 1968 Hope Publishing Company. All rights reserved. Used by permission.

184 © 1988 WGRG, The Iona Community (Glasgow, Scotland), G.I.A. Publications, Inc., Chicago, IL, exclusive agent.

186 © 1928 Oxford University Press, Walton St., Oxford OX2 6DP, England.

323 © Stainer & Bell. Used by permission of Hope Publishing Company. All rights reserved.

352 © 1963 Stainer & Bell. Used by permission of Hope Publishing Company.

364 Used by permission of Oxford University Press.

374 © 1982 Hope Publishing Company. All rights reserved. Used by permission.

379 © 1991 Jean Wiebe Janzen, 5508 E. Lane, Fresno, CA 93727, USA.

380 © 1987 Common Cup Company.

384 © 1927 *Homiletic and Pastoral Review,* published by Catholic Polls, Inc., c/o Kenneth Baker, 86 Riverside Dr., New York, NY 10024, USA.

465 © 1994 Herman G. Stuempfle, Jr., 330 Ridge Ave., Gettysburg, PA 17325, USA.

468 © 1975 Hope Publishing Company. All rights reserved. Used by permission.

475 © 1969 Hope Publishing Company. All rights reserved. Used by permission.

495 © 1994 Hope Publishing Company. All rights reserved. Used by permission.

583 © 1987 Walter Farquharson.

593 © 1969 Hope Publishing Company. All rights reserved. Used by permission.

598 © 1978 Desert Flower Music.

603 © 1983 Desert Flower Music. Used by permission.

614 © 1987 Sheila Johns, 38 Ruttan Bay, Winnipeg, MB R3T 0H6.

625 © 1933 National Adult School Organisation, MASU Centre, Gaywood Croft, Cregoe St., Birmingham B15 2ED, England.

670 © 1938 Unichappell Music, Inc., c/o Hal Leonard Publishing Corp., P.O. Box 13819, 7777 W. Bluemound Rd., Milwaukee, WI 53213, USA. Copyright renewed. Copyright secured. International copyright secured. All rights reserved.

673 © 1989 The Hymn Society. All rights reserved. Used by permission of Hope Publishing Company.

691 © 1974 Walter Farquharson.

703 © 1986 Hope Publishing Company. All rights reserved. Used by permission.

About the Authors

Stephen Adams is a member of First St. Andrew's United Church in London, Ontario. He is Associate Dean of Arts at the University of Western Ontario, where he teaches in the English Department. He is also active as a violinist and member of the church choir.

Judith A. Fetter was born in Winnipeg, Manitoba, and attended high school and university in Montreal. Married in 1959 to Rev. Lawrence Fetter, she accompanied him in ministry in Manitoba, Ontario, British Columbia, and finally for six years in northeast Brazil. Currently she is active in UCW and at presbytery and Conference levels, in the Conference Division of Global Concerns, and the Council of Canadians. Living in beautiful Victoria, she enjoys time to walk, cook, write, and make regular visits to two sons, one daughter, and seven grandchildren in Alberta and Ontario.

Heather Hemming serves the Leader-Sceptre Pastoral Charge in southwest Saskatchewan. A former geographer from the east coast, she is now enthralled with the prairie landscape.

Everett Hollis serves St. Andrew's Indian Head, Saskatchewan, where he resides with his life partner Ruth. A diversity of vocational and spiritual experiences have been and continue to be a major part of his life's journey.

Ian MacLean was born in the Maritimes and ordained in 1961. He has served congregations in Saskatchewan, New Brunswick, and Ontario. He is married to Wilma and they have three children and (at time of writing) two grandchildren.

Jessie McLeod is a retired Commissioned Minister living in Baddeck, Nova Scotia.

Fran Ota was born in Saskatchewan into a United Church minister's family and received a Bachelor of Music degree from the University of Manitoba in 1970. She went to Japan as a United Church missionary and married her language teacher, Norio, in 1971. She and her husband have lived in Vietnam, Australia, and the United States before coming to Toronto, and have four grown children. Fran has worked with refugees, as a community advisor, and as a language teacher. She worked at the United Church for five years and the Canadian Council of Churches for four years, and as an organist and choir director in Toronto. She received a Master of Divinity degree and was ordained in 1995, and presently serves Maxwell-McIntyre-Badjeros Pastoral Charge in Toronto Conference.

Don Parsons was a valued member of the Hymn-Worship Resource Committee, 1991-1996, as chair of the texts subcommittee related to the *Voices United* project. He has served in congregational life in five Ontario churches, including his current pastoral charge, Port Nelson United in Burlington. With his wife, Margaret, and two children, he shares love of music, theatre, and outdoor life.

Bernice Saulteaux has served the Hurricane Hills Pastoral Charge on Carry the Kettle Reserve since 1984. She received her training at the Dr. Jesse Saulteaux Centre.

Donna Sinclair is an active member of St. Andrew's United Church in North Bay, Ont. She is a senior writer with The United Church Observer and the author of several books dealing with matters of faith. At the time of writing, she was working on a collection of daily spiritual reflections for women.

Laura Sundberg serves the Wolseley-Sintaluta Pastoral Charge in Saskatchewan. She lives with her life partner Bill Ursel and their golden retriever Jonah in Wolseley.

Bob Wallace has been a minister in six provinces during the past forty years and is a Visiting Professor at the Atlantic School of Theology in Halifax and Acadia Divinity College in Wolfville, Nova Scotia. He has a particular interest in the relationship of faith and the arts.

Mac Watts recently retired from the Faculty of Theology at the University of Winnipeg, where he served for seven years as Dean of the Faculty, and was Associate Professor of Historical and Contemporary Theology. He chaired the two subcommittees in Winnipeg that did the basic work for *Services for Death and Burial* and *Pastoral Liturgies*. He has edited the journal *Touchstone* since its inception in 1983.

Voices United Resources

***Voices United:* The Hymn and Worship Book of The United Church of Canada** **$21.95**

Coming in June 1997:

Words Only Edition	**$18.95**
Music Leader's Edition (includes CD)	**$79.95**
Compact Disc	**$12.95**

***Voices United* Accessories:**

Sweatshirts

Burgundy Fruit of the Loom sweatshirts
with the logo in gold.

L 851 102 016	**$21.95**
XL 851 102 017	**$21.95**

Tote Bag

Sing with *Voices United*, share the joy of our new book
with this environmentally friendly canvas tote bag.

851 102 014 **$7.95 each**

Travel Mug

The car mates travel mug fits right into your car cup holder.
Almond colour with *Voices United* logo.

851 102 020 **$4.95 each**

AVAILABLE FROM:

United Church Distribution Centre
25 Connell Court, Unit 2
Etobicoke, ON M8Z 1E8
(416) 253-5456
Fax: (416) 253-1630

or your nearest Book Room

1-800-288-7365